ST LUCIA

THE MINI ROUGH GUIDE

D0752733

There are more than one hundred Rough Guide travel,
phrasebook, and music titles, covering destinations
from Amsterdam to Zimbabwe, languages from Czech
to Thai, and musics from World to Opera and Jazz

Forthcoming titles include

Cuba • Dominican Repubic
Las Vegas • Sardinia
Switzerland

Rough Guides on the Internet

www.roughguides.com

Rough Guide Credits

Text editor: Polly Thomas. Series editor: Mark Ellingham.
Typesetting: Justin Bailey and Link Hall.
Cartography: Ed Wright.
Picture research: Michelle Draycott.

Publishing Information

This first edition published September 1999 by
Rough Guides Ltd, 62–70 Shorts Gardens, London, WC2H 9AB

Distributed by the Penguin Group:

Penguin Books Ltd, 27 Wrights Lane, London W8 5TZ
Penguin Books USA Inc., 375 Hudson Street, New York 10014, USA
Penguin Books Australia Ltd, 487 Maroondah Highway,
PO Box 257, Ringwood, Victoria 3134, Australia
Penguin Books Canada Ltd, 10 Alcorn Avenue,
Toronto, Ontario, Canada M4V 1E4
Penguin Books (NZ) Ltd, 182–190 Wairau Road,
Auckland 10, New Zealand

Typeset in Bembo and Helvetica to an original design by Henry Iles.
Printed in Spain by Graphy Cems.

© Karl Luntta 272pp, includes index
A catalogue record for this book is available from the British Library.
ISBN 1-85828-329-9

The publishers and authors have done their best to
ensure the accuracy and currency of all the information
in *The Rough Guide to St Lucia*, however, they can accept
no responsibility for any loss, injury or inconvenience
sustained by any traveller as a result of information or
advice contained in the guide.

We set out to do something different when the first Rough Guide was published in 1982. Mark Ellingham, just out of university, was travelling in Greece. He brought along the popular guides of the day, but found they were all lacking in some way. They were either strong on ruins and museums but went on for pages without mentioning a beach or taverna. Or they were so conscious of the need to save money that they lost sight of Greece's cultural and historical significance. Also, none of the books told him anything about Greece's contemporary life – its politics, its culture, its people, and how they lived.

So with no job in prospect, Mark decided to write his own guidebook, one which aimed to provide practical information that was second to none, detailing the best beaches and the hottest clubs and restaurants, while also giving hard-hitting accounts of every sight, both famous and obscure, and providing up-to-the-minute information on contemporary culture. It was a guide that encouraged independent travellers to find the best of Greece, and was a great success, getting shortlisted for the Thomas Cook travel guide award, and encouraging Mark, along with three friends, to expand the series.

The Rough Guide list grew rapidly and the letters flooded in, indicating a much broader readership than had been anticipated, but one which uniformly appreciated the Rough Guide mix of practical detail and humour, irreverence and enthusiasm. Things haven't changed. The same four friends who began the series are still the caretakers of the Rough Guide mission today: to provide the most reliable, up-to-date and entertaining information to independent-minded travellers of all ages, on all budgets.

We now publish more than 100 titles and have offices in London and New York. The travel guides are written and researched by a dedicated team of more than 100 authors, based in Britain, Europe, the USA and Australia. We have also created a unique series of phrasebooks to accompany the travel series, along with an acclaimed series of music guides, and a best-selling pocket guide to the Internet and World Wide Web. We also publish comprehensive travel information on our Web site: **www.roughguides.com**

Help Us Update

We've gone to a lot of effort to ensure that this first edition of *The Rough Guide to St Lucia* is as up to date and accurate as possible. However, if you feel there are places we've underrated or over-praised, or find we've missed something good or covered something which has now gone, then please write: suggestions, comments or corrections are much appreciated.

We'll credit all contributions, and send a copy of the next edition (or any other Rough Guide if you prefer) for the best letters. Please mark letters: "Rough Guide St Lucia Update" and send to:

Rough Guides, 62–70 Shorts Gardens, London, WC2H 9AB, or
Rough Guides, 375 Hudson St, New York NY 10014.

Or send email to: **mail@roughguides.co.uk**
Online updates about this book can be found on
Rough Guides' Web site (see opposite)

The Author

Karl Luntta is the author of guides to Jamaica, the Virgin Islands and the Lesser Antilles, and writes on the islands for numerous publications. He is a newspaper columnist and has published fiction in *International Quarterly*, *Baltimore Review*, *North Atlantic Review* and other publications.

Acknowledgements

Thanks to Wenda and all at the St Lucia Tourist Board offices in Castries and Soufrière, and to Marcella Martinez, Laura Davidson and Marilyn Marx.

CONTENTS

The Guide

Listings

Contexts

Introduction

St **Lucia** more than lives up to the paradisal Caribbean stereotype: a glorious mix of honey sand beaches, translucent waters sheltering reefs swarming with tropical fish, lush interior rainforests, and a thriving culture that encompasses literature and theatre as well as music and dance. However, in contrast to other islands in the region, where the tourism infrastructure has been steadily expanding since the 1960s, St Lucia has only recently begun to attract visitors in any number. As a result, tourism has a much lower profile here, and this low-key feel is one of the island's biggest assets. With little of the jaded hustle that can mar more established Caribbean destinations, you'll find St Lucia a relaxed, informal and incredibly friendly place to visit. Despite the lack of hype, St Lucia's tourist facilities are top-notch, and, unusually, cater to all budgets – you can stay at luxury hotels or inexpensive guesthouses, dine in world-class restaurants or at roadside kiosks, and shop in large duty-free malls or at open air village markets.

You could spend an entire holiday exploring St Lucia's beaches, but you'd be missing out on the island's less obvious highlights. St Lucia's 616 square kilometres are ripe for exploration, and though a rental car is the optimum way to get around, bus links to most areas are good, and taxis are always available. If it is **beaches** you're after, you'll probably head first to the tourism strongholds of the **northwest coast**, where

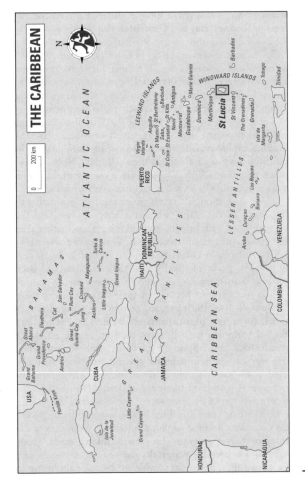

THE CARIBBEAN

N

0 ⊢————⊣ 200 km

ATLANTIC OCEAN

USA
Florida Keys
Grand Bahama
Great Abaco
Grand Providence
Andros
Eleuthera
Great Guana Cay
Cat
San Salvador
Rum Cay
Long
Crooked
Acklins
Little Inagua
Mayaguana
Turks & Caicos
Great Inagua

BAHAMAS

Isla de la Juventud
CUBA
Little Cayman
Grand Cayman

JAMAICA

GREATER ANTILLES

HAITI
DOMINICAN REPUBLIC
PUERTO RICO

Virgin Islands
Anguilla
St Martin
St Barthélemy
Saba
St Eustatius
St Croix
St Kitts
Nevis
Barbuda
Antigua
Montserrat

LEEWARD ISLANDS

Guadeloupe
Marie Galante
Dominica
Martinique

WINDWARD ISLANDS

St Lucia
St Vincent
The Grenadines
Grenada
Barbados
Tobago
Trinidad

LESSER ANTILLES

CARIBBEAN SEA

Aruba
Curaçao
Bonaire
Los Roques
Isla de Margarita

HONDURAS
NICARAGUA
COLOMBIA
VENEZUELA

scores of hotels and restaurants are clustered around the villages of **Rodney Bay** and **Gros Islet**. Reef-fringed swaths of white sand along this stretch of coastline justify its "Golden Mile" nickname. There's plenty of historical intrigue – as well as more idyllic seashores – at former pirate hangout and British military bastion **Pigeon Island**, and the remains of stone **forts** scattered throughout the area are a telling reminder of the fierce Anglo-French battles for possession of St Lucia, which saw the "Helen of the West Indies" change hands more than a dozen times. South of Rodney Bay, the bustling capital of **Castries** is also worth visiting, with its peaceful town square named after St Lucia's Nobel Prize-winning author Derek Walcott, and a clamorous, colourful market that provides a vivid insight into everyday island life.

These days, though, visitors are increasingly gravitating to the **south** of the island, where the pace is slower and the bays are lined with brightly painted fishing boats rather than the garish concrete of resort hotels. With a deep-water harbour framed by St Lucia's best-known landmark, the monolithic twin peaks of the **Pitons**, the attractive, laid-back town of **Soufrière** boasts gorgeous colonial architecture as well as unusual stretches of dark grey-brown volcanic sand. Within reach of the town are numerous managed attractions: sugarcane **plantations** established by French and English colonists have been opened up to the public or transformed into **botanical gardens**, while the bubbling, odorous La Soufrière **sulphur springs** have been re-packaged as the world's only drive-in volcano. These mineral-rich waters have been harnessed at nearby Diamond Estate, where you can take a restorative bathe in an outdoor pool.

Southern St Lucia is also the most convenient starting point for excursions into the rainforest-smothered mountains of the **interior forest reserves**. Laced with **hiking trails**, abundant with swimmable **waterfalls** and home to some rare and exotic **wildlife**, the forests provide an absorbing alternative to beach life. St Lucia's tropical environment is also showcased at the protected **nature reserves** along the southeast coast: the Fregate and Maria islands are home to magnificent frigate birds and endemic lizards, while pristine offshore reefs make for great snorkelling. Windswept, wild and pounded by the Atlantic Ocean, the spectacular beaches of the east coast are better for hiking than for swimming, and **leatherback turtles** visit more regularly than tourists.

A fusion of French, British and African traditions, St Lucia's Creole **culture** is an intriguing mix: while the official language is English, the lingua franca is a mellifluous, French-based Patois that employs African vocabulary and structures. Similarly, the local cuisine blends French traditions with island ingredients, focusing on local seafood and root crops originally imported from Africa on slave ships. However, the most conspicuous – and exciting – expression of St Lucia's culture are its **festivals**, Christian in origin but African in character. **Carnival** is by far the biggest event, a colourful, animated round of frenetic parties, calypso contests and parades of revellers decked out in wild costumes portraying spirits and devils. If you're not lucky enough to be in St Lucia for Carnival, or for the more intimate summer saints' festivals, the St Lucian propensity for partying is indulged each Friday when the tiny village of Gros Islet is overtaken by a classic West Indian "jump up", a **street party** where tourists and locals alike descend for a night of eating, drinking and dancing under the stars. St Lucia's fastest-growing event, the annual **Jazz Festival** is a more sophisticated gathering, with some of the genre's biggest names performing under the palm trees of Pigeon Island.

When to go

For many visitors, St Lucia's biggest attraction is its tropical **climate**. During the December to April high season, the island is pleasantly hot, with little rain and constant northeasterly trade winds keeping the nights cool. Temperatures rise even further during the summer months, which can also be wet: the rainy season lasts from June to October, and during this time, short, heavy bursts of rain are matched by an increase in humidity; rainfall is nearly three times heavier in the central rainforests than along the coast. The rainy months also coincide with the **hurricane season**, which runs roughly from late August to October.

As you'd expect, St Lucia is busiest in the first few months of the year; during this time, some beaches, particularly those in the northwest, are likely to be crowded, and hotel prices are at their peak. In the mid-April to mid-December low season, accommodation rates, airfares and even car rental prices can decrease significantly.

St Lucia's climate

| | °F | | °C | | Rainfall | |
| | Average daily | | Average daily | | Average monthly | |
	MAX	MIN	MAX	MIN	IN	MM
Jan	82	69	28	21	5.3	135
Feb	83	69	28	21	3.6	91
March	84	69	29	21	3.8	97
April	87	71	31	22	3.4	96
May	88	73	31	23	5.9	150
June	88	74	31	23	8.6	218
July	87	74	31	23	9.3	236
Aug	88	74	31	23	10.6	269
Sept	88	73	31	23	9.9	252
Oct	87	72	31	22	9.3	236
Nov	85	71	29	22	9.1	231
Dec	83	70	28	21	7.8	798

BASICS

Getting there from Britain and Ireland

The great majority of British and Irish visitors to St Lucia arrive on a **direct charter flight** as part of a package holiday – and even if you plan to travel independently this is still the cheapest way to get here. Charters do have limitations, however, notably a fixed return date of one, two or a maximum three weeks.

When it comes to direct **scheduled flights**, the choice is limited: Virgin fly once a week direct from London Gatwick; BWIA (British West Indian Airline) depart twice weekly from London Heathrow; and BA have two flights a week via Bridgetown, Barbados.

Fares and airlines

The **cost** of a flight to St Lucia varies widely, depending on the time of year. High season is from July until the end of August, low season from September until the end of April, and shoulder season from May until the end of June.

Tickets sold by **travel agents** (see the box on p.5) tend to be much cheaper than those bought direct from the airlines, while the cheapest tickets of all are sold by **discount operators**; check travel ads in the weekend papers, the holiday pages of ITV's Teletext and, in London, *Time Out* and the *Evening Standard*. Giveaway magazines aimed at young travellers, like *TNT*, are also useful resources.

Your cheapest **charter option** is likely to be Caledonian Airways, which fly roughly three times a week from London Gatwick with fares ranging from £207 during the shoulder and low seasons to £580 in the high season. Virgin's direct **scheduled flight** from London Gatwick on Sunday costs around £350 during the low season, rising to £775 at the height of the high season. Virgin also fly non-stop to Barbados (Mon, Thurs & Sat) and Antigua (Wed & Fri), with a connecting flight on local airline LIAT to St Lucia. BWIA has a twice-weekly service (Tues & Sun) from Heathrow (starting at £301 in low season, £783 in high season). **British Airways** also fly twice a week from London Gatwick (Mon & Sat), touching down in Bridgetown; their fare is from £495 in low season to £580 in high season; minimum stay is seven nights.

Flights from **regional airports** in the UK all go via London Gatwick: BA fly from Manchester (£550 low season, £755 high season) and Glasgow (£550 low season, £755 high season) via Gatwick to St Lucia. Delta also goes from Manchester via Gatwick (£490 low season, £631 high season); and from Belfast there is a Jersey European flight to Gatwick, then on to St Lucia with Virgin Atlantic (£590 low season, £810 high season).

Both BA and Virgin fly twice-weekly from **Dublin** to St Lucia via London Gatwick; their high-season fares are around Ir£770, but BA's low season fare is lower than Virgin's, at Ir£462 as opposed to Ir£686.

Lastly, if you plan to indulge in some **island hopping** around the Caribbean from St Lucia, BWIA or LIAT air passes can be worthwhile (see p.16).

Airlines

British Airways ℡0345/222111, *www.british-airways.com*.
BWIA ℡0171/745 1100, *www.bwee.com*.

Caledonian Airways ℡01293/567800.
Delta ℡0800/414767, *www.deltaairlines.com*.
Virgin Atlantic ℡01293/747747, *www.flyvirgin.com/atlantic*.

Discount travel agents

Bridge the World, 47 Chalk Farm Rd, London NW1 8AN
℡0171/916 0990.
Cheap Flights, *www.cheapflights.co.uk*.
Co-op Travel Care, 35 Belmont Rd, Belfast 4 ℡01232/471 717.
Council Travel, 28a Poland St, London W1V 3DB
℡0171/437 7767.
Flightbookers, 177–178 Tottenham Court Rd, London W1P
0LX ℡0171/757 2444; plus branches in Glasgow and at
Gatwick Airport.
Joe Walsh Tours, 34 Grafton St, Dublin 2 ℡01/671 8751;
other branches throughout Dublin and in Cork.
The London Flight Centre, 131 Earls Court Rd, London
SW5 9RH ℡0171/244 6411; plus other branches in London.
North South Travel, Moulsham Mill Centre, Parkway,
Chelmsford, Essex CM2 7PX ℡01245/492882.
STA Travel, 86 Old Brompton Rd, London SW7 3LH;
117 Euston Rd, London NW1 2SX;
38 Store St, London WC1E 7BZ; ℡0171/361 6262;
branches in Aberdeen, Birmingham, Bristol, Cambridge,
Canterbury, Cardiff, Coventry, Durham, Glasgow, Leeds,
Loughborough, Manchester, Oxford, Nottingham,
Sheffield and Warwick.
Trailfinders, 42–50 Earls Court Rd, London W8 6FT
℡0171/937 5400; 4–5 Dawson St, Dublin 2 ℡01/677 7888;
plus branches in Birmingham, Bristol, Glasgow and
Manchester.
The Travel Bug, 125a Gloucester Rd, London SW7 4SF
℡0171/835 2000; 597 Cheetham Hill Rd, Manchester M8 5EJ
℡0161/721 4000.

Usit, Fountain Centre, College St, Belfast BT1 6ET
℡01232/324073; 19 Aston Quay, Dublin 2 ℡01/602 1700;
plus branches in Cork, Derry, Galway, Limerick and Waterford.
Usit CAMPUS, 52 Grosvenor Gardens, London SW1W 0AG
℡0171/730 8111; plus branches in Birmingham, Brighton,
Bristol, Cambridge, Edinburgh, Glasgow, Manchester,
Oxford and Dublin.

Packages

St Lucia is a popular **package tour** destination, and there
is a wealth of operators to choose from with accommodation ranging from self-catering apartments to full-on
luxury hotels: a selection is given opposite. Virgin Holidays offer amongst the cheapest deals; they have an
all-inclusive week-long break starting at £789, including
transfers. Thomas Cook offers similar all-inclusive packages, with special deals available for honeymooners and
repeat visitors. In Ireland, Joe Walsh has departures from
Dublin, Cork and Shannon, with onward BWIA connections via Heathrow; prices start at £959 per week,
all-inclusive.

Many operators also offer special deals for couples want-
ing to **get married** on St Lucia: Sunday departures leave
time for you to apply for your marriage licence in time for
the big event on the following Saturday. Tropical Places has
a special weddings leaflet listing tailor-made deals – if you
stay at your hotel for fourteen days, they may arrange your
nuptials for free.

Finally, Caribbean Escapes operate a seven-day
"Caribbean Chic" **cruise**, starting at £3095, which departs
from Palm Beach and stops at St Lucia en route to
Barbados. Details of more cruises leaving from Miami are
listed on pp.11–12.

Tour operators

Caribbean Escapes ©0171/581 3517, fax 589 1468, *caribbeanescapes@caribtours.demon.co.uk*.
Caribbean Journeys ©0171/849 4011, fax 849 4253, *www.worldwide-journeys.com*.
Hayes & Jarvis ©0181/748 5050, fax 741 0299.
Joe Walsh Tours ©01/6763053, fax 676 6572.
Kuoni ©01306/740888, fax 744222, *www.kuoni.co.uk*.
Thomas Cook ©08705/666222, fax 01733/412921, *www.tch.thomascook.com*.
Tropical Places ©01342/825123, fax 822364 *www.tropical.co.uk*.
Virgin Holidays ©01293/617181 fax 536957, *www.virgin-hols.co.uk*.

Getting there from North America

If you're travelling from North America, **flying** is obviously the most practical way of getting to St Lucia, and in testament to the island's growing popularity as a holiday destination, international airlines have consistently increased their flight schedules over the years. During the high season, flights are on a daily basis, with services only slightly reduced in the low season.

Fares and airlines

Though the Caribbean draws visitors year-round, airline **fares** vary according to season, with the busiest period from mid-December to mid-April. During this **high season**, you can generally expect higher airfares, hotel rates and even car rental prices. Having said that, there are often great deals to be had in high season, particularly if you're able to travel at the weekend. During the **low season**, which comprises most of the rest of the year, accommodation rates are generally at their lowest but airfares fluctuate depending on the airline. Some airlines also adjust their fares during the spring and autumn **shoulder seasons**, when prices lie somewhere between low and high season rates.

Shopping for flights, your first move should be to call the airlines direct (see opposite); it's a good idea to phone more than once – odds are you'll get a different agent each time, and possibly a better quote. It's also worth calling travel agents that specialize in the Caribbean (reliable outlets are listed on p.10). These often offer good deals on flights, particularly when you book a package that includes accommodation.

A typical **scheduled return fare** from New York JFK starts at US$620 in the high season, and in the low season ranges from US$580 to US$640. With four months advance purchase, both these fares could be reduced to as little as US$300. It's also worth bearing in mind that you may pay as much as US$80 more if you choose to fly to George F.L. Charles Airport in Castries rather than the main international airport, Hewanorra, in the south of the island.

Charter companies also operate regular direct flights from North America to St Lucia, with fares running somewhat lower than scheduled flights. The disadvantage is that charter airlines usually have set departure and return dates, which limits your flexibility. It's also worth bearing in mind that charter airlines have been known to cancel flights that aren't filled, sometimes with less than satisfactory reimbursement to ticket holders, and that schedules may change without warning. One of the more frequent and reliable carriers is GWV International, which offers three-, four-, and seven-night charter/package deals (you must stay at a designated hotel) during the high season. However, you cannot contact GWV directly (though the Web site listed below gives schedules), and all of their flights and packages must be booked through travel agents.

Lastly, if you plan to indulge in some **island hopping** around the Caribbean from St Lucia, BWIA or LIAT air passes can be worthwhile (see p.16).

Airlines

Air Canada in US ✆1-800/776-3000, in Canada 800/268-7240, *www.aircanada.ca*. Flights from Toronto to Barbados and Antigua, with connections to St Lucia.
Air Jamaica ✆1-800/523-5585, *www.airjamaica.com*.
Several direct flights a week from New York to Hewanorra, plus services via Jamaica from Atlanta, Baltimore, Chicago, Philadelphia, Los Angeles, Fort Lauderdale, Miami and Newark.
American Airlines ✆1-800/433-7300, *www.aa.com*.
Daily flights to Hewanorra from major cities via Miami.
From San Juan in Puerto Rico, AA's subsidiary American Eagle (✆1-800/433-7300) connects daily to George F.L. Charles Airport.
BWIA ✆1-800/327-7401, *www.bwiacaribbean.com*.
Several direct flights per week from Miami and New York, via Antigua.
Canadian Royal Airlines ✆877/769-2524, *www.royalairlines.com*. Flights from several Canadian cities; schedules change regularly.
GWV No phone, *www.gwvtravel.com*.

Sunquest Vacations ©416/485-1700, *www.sunquest.ca*. Toronto-based charter airline with occasional flights to St Lucia; schedules change regularly.

Discount travel agents and consolidators

Air Courier Association ©1-800/282-1202 or 303/278-8810, *www.aircourier.org*.
STA Travel ©1-800/777-0112, *www.sta-travel.com*; branches in New York, San Francisco, Boston, Miami, Chicago, Seattle, Philadelphia and Washington DC.
Travel Avenue ©1-800/333-3335 or 312/876-6866, *www.tipc.com*.
Travel CUTS ©1-800/667-2887 (in Canada) or ©416/979-2406, *www.travelcuts.com*.
Worldtek Travel ©1/800-243-1723, *www.worldtek.com*.

Packages

Package trips to St Lucia can be a good deal, often costing less than the sum of flights and accommodation bought separately, and sometimes including extras such as a rental car. Specialist trips are also available, focusing on activities such as scuba diving. You'll often have to stay for at least three nights and take a set number of meals in the hotel, but the savings can be significant. When booking packages, however, remember that most rates are quoted per person based upon two people sharing a room. The fare for a single traveller is often more than half of that of a pair of travellers.

Package trips can be arranged through any of the tour operators listed opposite; or contact one of the agents listed above, who should be able to search out a deal that suits your budget and any special interests. It's also worth scanning the Sunday travel sections of large city newspapers, where special deals often appear. Package **prices** can vary considerably, depending on the class of your accommodation (all-inclusives, for example, will obviously cost more), but two people sharing a room can expect to pay from US$1200 to $2000 per person for flights and a week's accommodation during the high season, and from US$900 to $1500 per person in the low season.

Tour operators

Air Jamaica Vacations ©1-800/523-5585, *www.airjamaica.com*.
American Airlines Vacations ©1-800/774-8993, *www.aa.com*.
Empress Travel and Cruises ©212/688-5800, *www.epmresstrvl.com*.
Liberty Travel ©212/580-7100, *www.libertytravel.com*.
Massachusetts Audubon Society ©1-800/289-9504, *www.massaudubon.org*.

Cruises

Cruises are a popular way to visit – albeit briefly – a number of Caribbean destinations, with trips lasting three days, six to nine days or ten or more days. The average length of stay in a port is a day or less. Rates are based on "inside" or "outside" cabins (with or without ocean view, respectively), for one or two persons per cabin. Most Caribbean cruises depart from Miami, Fort Lauderdale or Tampa or San Juan, Puerto Rico.

Cruise lines listed overleaf are among the most popular with St Lucia as a destination. Typical rates given are for an inside cabin in high season, excluding port fees (US$120–165) and any airfare.

Cruise lines

Carnival Cruise Lines ✆1-800/327-9501. US$1000 (7 days); US$1437 (10 days).
Celebrity Cruise Lines ✆1-800/437-3111. US$1555 (7 days); US$2645 (10 days).
Holland America Line ✆1-800/847-8701. US$2000 (14 days).
Princess Cruises ✆1-800/421-0522. US$1308 (7 days).

Getting there from Australia and New Zealand

The Caribbean is not a bargain destination from **Australia** or **New Zealand**. With no direct flights to St Lucia, the only way to get there is to take a flight to one of the main gateway US airports, and pick up onward connections from there.

Generally, the least expensive and most straightforward routes are via New York or Miami. Both are served by regular flights to George F.L. Charles Airport in Castries and to Hewanorra airport in Vieux Fort. If you're planning to see St Lucia as part of a longer trip, **round-the-world** (RTW) tickets are worth considering, as they're usually better value than a simple return flight. Whatever kind of ticket you're after, your first move should be to call one of the specialist agents listed on p.14 – they can fill you in on all the latest fares and special offers. If you're a **student** or under 26, you may be able to undercut some of the prices given here; STA Travel is a good place to start.

Fares and air passes

From **Australia**, the most direct **routes** you're likely to find are the Air New Zealand, United and Qantas regular services to Los Angeles, with connecting flights to New York or Miami with American Airlines or United, from where you connect to St Lucia flights. Return **fares** to New York or Miami from the eastern states of **Australia** on any of these airlines (excluding taxes) cost from A$2230 in the low season and A$3500 in the high season. If you're not in a hurry, Japan Airlines have cheaper fares to New York from Sydney via an overnight stop in Tokyo for A$1800; South African Airways fly to Miami via Johannesburg for A$2199 from Perth, A$2299 from Sydney. Point-to-point return fares from Sydney to St Lucia (via the USA) cost around A$3500. Onward flights from New York or Miami to St Lucia are available with BWIA (see p.9 for more on connections from North America). If you plan to indulge in some **island hopping** around the Caribbean, BWIA or LIAT air passes can be worthwhile (see p.16).

From **New Zealand**, Air New Zealand, United and Qantas fly to Los Angeles with connections on to Miami or New York; through fares to Miami start at NZ$2800 in the low season and NZ$3800 in the high season, also exclusive of taxes. Flights to St Lucia from Auckland (via the USA) cost from NZ$3800.

Travel agents

Anywhere Travel, 345 Anzac Parade, Kingsford, Sydney, ⊙02/9663 0411, *anywhere@ozemail.com.au.*

Budget Travel, 6 Fort St, Auckland ⊙09/366 0061 or ⊙0800/808040.

Destinations Unlimited, 3 Milford Rd, Milford, Auckland ⊙09/373 4033.

Flight Centres Australia: Level 11, 33 Berry St, North Sydney ⊙13 1600 or 13 3133 (24hr), plus branches nationwide. New Zealand: National Bank Towers, 205–225 Queen St, Auckland ⊙09/209 6171, plus branches nationwide. *www.flightcentre.com.*

STA Travel Australia: 855 George St, Sydney ⊙02/9212 1255; 256 Flinders St, Melbourne ⊙03/9654 7266; nearest branch ⊙13 1776, telesales ⊙1300/360 960. New Zealand: 10 High St, Auckland ⊙09/309 0458, telesales ⊙09/366 6673, plus branches in Wellington, Christchurch, Dunedin, Palmerston North, Hamilton. *www.statravelaus.com.au.*

Thomas Cook Australia: 175 Pitt St, Sydney; 257 Collins St, Melbourne, plus branches (local branch ⊙13 1771, telesales ⊙1800/063 913). New Zealand: Level 5, Telstra Business Centre, Auckland, ⊙09/359 5200.

Trailfinders, 8 Spring St, Sydney ⊙02/9247 7666.

Travel.com, 80 Clarence St, Sydney ⊙02/9290 1500. *www.travel.com.au.*

RTW tickets

Given these fares and routings, **round-the-world tickets** that take in one of the gateway airports in the United States are worth considering, especially if you have the time to make the most of a few stopovers.

Ultimately, your choice of route will depend on where else you want to visit besides St Lucia. Various airlines offer routings including stops in New York or Miami from A\$1999/NZ\$2699. The Global Explorer and One World tickets from British Airways, Qantas and American Airlines take in several Caribbean destinations, with routings offered on a mileage basis. A sample itinerary starting in Sydney or Melbourne and flying to Los Angeles, San Juan, St Lucia, Barbados, London, Bangkok and back to Sydney or Melbourne starts from around A\$2500/ NZ\$3090. Call any of the agents or airlines listed for more information.

Airlines

Air New Zealand Australia ℗13 2476;
New Zealand ℗09/357 3000.
American Airlines Australia ℗1300/650 747.
British West Indies Airlines (BWIA) Australia ℗02/9285 6811;
New Zealand ℗09/309 8094.
Japan Airlines Australia ℗02/9272 1111;
New Zealand ℗09/379 9906.
Qantas Australia ℗13 1211; New Zealand ℗09/357 8900 or 0800/808 767.
South African Airways Australia ℗02/9223 4402;
New Zealand ℗09/309 9132.
United Airlines Australia ℗13 1777;
New Zealand ℗09/379 3800.

Packages and cruises

Package holidays to St Lucia from Australia and New Zealand are few and far between, and many specialists act as agents for US-based operators, simply adding a return flight from Australia onto the cost. **Cruises** account for a large sector of the market: most depart from Miami or Fort Lauderdale, and because prices are based on US dollar amounts, they fluctuate with the exchange rate. To give some idea, all-inclusive eleven-day cruises calling at seven islands including St Lucia start at A\$880 (A\$2870 including airfare from Australia). The luxury end of the market is catered for by Caribbean Destinations and Contours, both of which offer resort- and villa-based holidays as well as cruises, with a choice of accommodation in St Lucia – mostly in self-contained resort complexes. Prices start at around A\$4000 for 14 days, based on low-season airfares from Australia and two people sharing a room.

Specialist agents and tour operators

Caribbean Destinations, Level 1, North Tower, The Rialto, 525 Collins St, Melbourne ℡1800/354 104.
Contours, 466 Victoria St, North Melbourne ℡03/9670 6900.
Mediterranean Shipping Cruises, Level 8, 155 George St, Sydney ℡1800/028 502.
Wiltrans, Level 10, 189 Kent St, Sydney ℡02/9255 0899.

Caribbean island hopping

It's not difficult to use St Lucia as a launchpad for visits to **other Caribbean islands**. Flying is naturally the fastest way to do it, and several pan-Caribbean airlines ply routes between the islands, with daily services (not necessarily non-stop) to and from St Lucia. Make sure you carry your passport or identification when you fly, and an outward ticket for departing St Lucia. Ferry services between some Eastern Caribbean islands are also worth considering; they take a little longer, but are less expensive than flying. To organize your island hopping, call the airlines directly before you leave or in St Lucia – numbers are listed overleaf; once there, you can also call in at one of the local travel agents listed on p.218.

Flights

George F.L. Charles Airport in Castries is the base of **HelenAir**, St Lucia's national airline, which flies direct to Trinidad, Dominica, Grenada, Barbados and St Vincent and the Grenadines. Return flights range from EC$280 to $400. You'll also find ticket counters here for the American Airlines subsidiary **American Eagle**, which flies daily to San Juan with onward connections to major North American cities. American Eagle makes connections from St Lucia to most Caribbean islands via its San Juan hub; main destinations include St Thomas, St Croix, St Maarten, Anguilla, Dominican Republic, Aruba, Grenada and St Kitts; round-trip fares average at just below the EC$1000 mark. **British West Indies Airways (BWIA)** connects St Lucia to Trinidad and Tobago, Antigua, Barbados, Jamaica, Grenada, St Martin, Caracas and Guyana, as well as New York and Miami; again, round-trip fares average at around EC$1000. Based in Antigua, **Leeward Islands Air Transport (LIAT)** is one of the Caribbean's busiest carriers, though not always the most efficient, flying to nearly every island in the Eastern Caribbean, and non-stop from St Lucia to Antigua, Barbados, Martinique, Trinidad and St Vincent.

Return fares range from EC$296 to nearby St Vincent, to EC$748 to St Thomas in the US Virgin Islands. **Air Martinique** services St Martin and Martinique. From St Lucia, sample return fares (exclusive of taxes) include EC$282 to Martinique on Air Martinique, and EC$389 to Barbados on LIAT.

Airlines

Air Martinique ©452-2463 or 453-6660.
American Airlines In UK © 0345/789789;
in US ©1-800/433-7300; in St Lucia ©454-6777.
American Eagle in St Lucia ©452-1820.
Air Jamaica in UK ©0181/570 7999; in US ©1-800/523-5585;
in St Lucia ©453-6611.
BWIA in UK ©0171/745 1100; in US ©1-800/327-7401;
in St Lucia ©452 3778.
HelenAir in St Lucia ©452-1958.
LIAT in St Lucia ©452 2348 or 452-3056.

Air passes

If you're planning to visit more than a couple of islands, it's worth considering a **multi-destination ticket**, such as those offered by **LIAT**. Their Caribbean Super Explorer costs US$475 plus applicable departure taxes (averaging US$10) and allows unlimited travel for twenty days to any LIAT destination (one stopover per destination). The scaled-back Explorer fare allows three stopovers within twenty days with return to your point of origin for US$265 plus taxes. Discounts are offered for senior citizens and children. Contact LIAT through your travel agent at home, or call them once you arrive (©452-2348 or 452-3056). Bear in mind, however, that schedules can be unreliable so it's important to reconfirm all flights.

Trinidad-based **BWIA** offer similar **island-hopper fares** from time to time, allowing multiple stops within a set time period. However, availability is sporadic – check with your local travel agent or call for current information once in St Lucia (©452-3778 or 452-3789).

Ferries

St Lucia's closest neighbours are easily accessible by **sea**. The **L'Express des Iles** high-speed passenger ferry currently leaves Castries for Guadeloupe four times per week (Mon 5pm, Tues 1.50pm, Sat 7am, Sun 1pm; 1hr 20min), stopping at Martinique and Dominica en route. In addition to a departure tax of EC$20, you'll pay EC$414 for a round-trip ticket, which allows a stop in Martinique or Dominica at no extra cost. A ten percent discount is available to those under 26 or over 60. The ferry is represented by Cox and Company in Castries – for information and latest schedules, call ©452-2211.

Visas and red tape

Citizens of Britain, the US and Canada can enter St Lucia without a **visa** and stay for up to 42 days; longer stays must be arranged through the St Lucia immigration department (©454-6239) once on the island. You'll need to produce either a passport or photo identification such as a driver's licence plus proof of citizenship (birth certificate or residency card, for example). On production of a passport, citizens of Ireland, Australia, New Zealand and all Commonwealth countries can enter without a visa and stay for up to 28 days, after which you have to apply to the St Lucia immigration department. Overall, it's best for citizens of all countries to travel with a passport.

All visitors are required to show a ticket for onward travel, and you'll have to indicate where you'll be staying on St Lucia, although this doesn't mean you can't move to different accommodation. For **enquiries**, call the St Lucia immigration department (see p.19) or St Lucian embassies or consulates in your own country.

St Lucian embassies and high commissions abroad

UK

10 Kensington Court, London W8 5DI ✆0171/937 9522, fax 0171/937 8704.

Canada

112 Kent St, Suite 1610, Ottawa, Ontario K1P 5P2 ✆613/236-8952, fax 613/236-3042.

USA

3216 New Mexico Ave NW, Washington DC 20016 ✆202/364-6792, fax 202/364-6723.

There is no St Lucian diplomatic representation in Australia, New Zealand or Ireland.

For details of foreign embassies and consulates in St Lucia, see p.216.

Information and maps

The **St Lucia Tourist Board** maintains several offices abroad, and it's worth contacting them to pick up general information and free maps before you leave. They also hand out hotel brochures, though they can't make reservations for you.

For the best on-island information, contact the main office of the St Lucia Tourist Board at the Pointe Seraphine complex in Castries (PO Box 221, Castries, St Lucia, WI ℡452-4094 or 452-5968, fax 453-1121, *slutour@candw.lc*). There are also **tourist board kiosks** at George F.L. Charles Airport, the La Place Carenage and Pointe Seraphine shopping complexes in Castries (see p.56, p.63 and p.64), at Hewanorra airport (see p.111) in Vieux Fort, and at the waterfront in Soufrière (see p.101).

Another useful source of up-to-date local information are the free, visitor-oriented publications available from the tourist board and from hotels across the island. *Tropical Traveller* is a monthly tabloid geared towards tourists, with lots of articles and suggestions for things to do as well as restaurant and nightclub listings, while the glossy magazine *Visions*, published by the St Lucia Hotel and Tourism Association, offers more of the same with the addition of hotel listings. It's also worth browsing the **Internet** for island information, and we've recommended some of the most useful sites on p.23.

St Lucian Tourist offices abroad

Canada
8 King St East, Suite 700, Toronto, Ontario M5C 1B5
℡416/362-4242, fax 362-7832, *sltbcda@netcom.ca*.

United Kingdom
421a Finchley Rd, London NW3 6HJ, ☎0171/431 3675,
fax 431-7920, *destination@pwaxis.com.uk*.

USA
820 2nd Ave, 9th Floor, New York, NY 10017, ☎1-800/456-3984
or 212/867-2950, fax 212/867-2795, *info@st-lucia.com*.

Maps

Though tourist offices (and even car rental companies) will
provide adequate **maps** of St Lucia, you may get a more
useful and detailed map from suppliers at home. The best
available is the 1:50,000 Ordnance Survey tourist map, available from bookshops or map specialists. In the UK, try
Stanfords, 12–14 Long Acre, London, WC2E 9LP (for mail
order call ☎0171/836 1321), and in the US, try Rand
McNally – for mail order or your nearest outlet call ☎1-
800/333-0136 (ext 2111). In St Lucia, the Lands and
Surveys department in the government complex at the
north end of Peynier Street in Castries (Mon–Fri
8.30am–noon & 1.30–2pm; ☎452-2611 ext 7156) have the
1:50,000 map as well as a three-part series covering the
northern, middle and southern sections of the country
(1:25,000 scale), as well as a good city map of Castries.

St Lucia on the net

St Lucia Tourist Board
www.stlucia.org
The best general site, with history and travel facts as well as
information on activities, hotels, restaurants, tourist office
contacts on the island and overseas, product lines manufactured
in St Lucia and tips for those planning a St Lucian wedding.

Government of St Lucia
www.stlucia.gov.lc
Quick-loading site with all the statistics you'd ever want to know plus government news.

Ethnologue: St Lucia
www.sil.org/ethnologue/countries/StLu.html
Discussion of St Lucian Patois, its origins and its relation to other Caribbean French-based Patois languages.

St Lucia Jazz Festival
stluciajazz.com
Listings of yearly line-ups with artist biographies, news, current schedules and information on hotels and travel.

St Lucia Hotel and Tourism Association
www.stluciatravel.com.lc
The official site of the SLHTA, including a long list of hotels and restaurants, duty-free shops and activities, as well as current weather reports.

St Lucia One Stop
www.sluonestop.com
Lively site with a chat room, searchable St Lucia phone directory and links to local newspapers. Worth a look is the link to "Cooking with Kouly", a locally televised cooking show, where you'll find recipes and jokes.

ST LUCIA ON THE NET

Health and insurance

Visitors to St Lucia are unlikely to suffer any real **health problems**. **Tap water** is usually safe to drink, except in the immediate aftermath of hurricanes and heavy rains, when the potable water supply can be contaminated. In any case, inexpensive bottled water is available in supermarkets and shops. Under no circumstances should you drink river water – it might be okay, but assume that it's not. Bilharzia, a blood fluke that can cause serious liver, spleen and artery damage, has been found in rivers and streams on the island.

Your main health risk is probably the **tropical sun**, which is extremely strong, even on cloudy days. A wide-brimmed hat and strong sunscreen will help protect you, and if you are light-skinned and plan on snorkelling for any length of time, wearing a good-quality T-shirt (UV rays can penetrate thin clothing) will guard against overexposing your back. To avoid dehydration and sunstroke, you should aim to drink at least four litres of water per day, and keep covered up with light cotton clothing while out hiking or exploring, especially between 11am and 3pm, when the sun's at its strongest.

The only other risk that travellers are likely to encounter are the poisonous **manchineel trees** with their shiny, green leaves, widespread along St Lucian shorelines. These should be treated with extreme caution as both the fruit, resembling a small, yellow apple, and the milky sap are toxic. Avoid touching any part of the tree or even taking cover under its boughs during a rain shower – the runoff can cause burns. Most hotels have labelled manchineels on their grounds.

AIDS is present in St Lucia, making it extremely foolish to engage in unsafe sex. However, despite health education programmes, taboos still exist regarding condom use and other safe sex practices. You can buy condoms on the island, but as they may have been sitting on shelves for a while, it's advisable to bring your own.

Medical help and insurance

If you are unfortunate enough to need **medical help** in St Lucia, there are hospitals and health clinics throughout the island, but they are likely to be crowded and the facilities limited. Most large hotels can recommend a doctor but for anything serious you will want to go elsewhere.

Details of hospitals, medical centres and pharmacies in St Lucia are given on p.216 and p.217.

It's a good idea to take out **travel insurance** before you leave for St Lucia, preferably a policy that covers medical treatment (including evacuation), theft and loss of baggage. Most travel agents and tour operators will offer you insurance when you book your flight or holiday, but it pays to shop around and check what cover you may already have. Home insurance policies may cover theft or loss whilst overseas, and private medical insurance may also be valid abroad; if this applies, make sure that you know how to claim. If you plan to indulge in **watersports** such as scuba diving, you'll often pay a higher premium, and it might be more difficult to find an appropriate policy. Also, bear in mind that some insurance companies will not cover **travellers over 65**, and those that do are likely to charge hefty premiums.

Note that in the event of a medical emergency you'll need a police report to make an insurance claim. Also, you will have to pay for any small medical bills and be reimbursed at home, so be sure to keep receipts.

In **Britain and Ireland**, travel insurance schemes are sold by almost every travel agent or bank, and by specialist insurance companies. The cost will depend on what you want to be insured for, and for how long: for around £35–50, you should find a policy offering two weeks' cover for cancellation and curtailment of flights, medical expenses, travel delay, accident, missed departures, lost baggage, lost passport, personal liability and legal expenses.

In **North America**, expect to pay about US$120 per week for a package covering medical, evacuation, accident and loss of life.

In **Australia** and **New Zealand**, policies covering St Lucia cost around A$189 or NZ$220 for one month, and A$295 or NZ$330 for two months. Cover More and Ready Plan both offer insurance.

Travel insurance companies

Britain and Ireland

Age Concern ✆01883/346964
Campus ✆0171/730 8111
Columbus Travel Insurance ✆0171/375 0011
Endsleigh Insurance ✆0171/436 4451
Marcus Hearne & Co Ltd ✆0171/739 3444
STA ✆0171/361 6262
Worldwide ✆01732/773366

North America

Access America International ✆1-800/284-8300
American Express ✆1-800/234-0375
Carefree Travel Insurance ✆1-800/323-3149
Desjardins Travel Insurance (Canada) ✆1-800/463-7830

Travel Guard ✆1-800/826-1300, *www.noelgroup.com*
Travel Insurance Services ✆1-800/937-1387

Australia and New Zealand

Cover More ✆02/9202 8000 & 1800/251 881
Ready Plan Australia ✆03/9791 5077 & 1800/337 462;
New Zealand ✆09/379 3208

Getting around

How easy you'll find it to **get around** St Lucia depends very much on where you want to go. While the more populated parts of the island – the west coast, for example – are well connected by buses, the northwest coast around Pointe du Cap and the east coast north of Dennery, where roads are poor, are only accessible to those with their own transport.

If you're laid-back enough to cope with waiting time and frequent stops along the route, travelling by **bus** is probably the most convenient and economical way to get around, with fares averaging out at EC$8 or less. An alternative is to rent **taxis**, though fares can soon add up.

The ideal way to get around is, of course, to rent a **car**. As well as giving you complete independence, it's ultimately less expensive than taxi travel if you intend to really explore the island. If a car is beyond your budget, though, and you have the nerve, renting a **motorbike** is worth considering, though this isn't exactly the safest way of getting around. To drive a car or ride a motorbike on the island, visitors must purchase a temporary St Lucian **licence**. Valid for three months, these cost EC$54 and are issued by rental companies on production of a valid licence (or an international permit) from your own country of origin. Remember that in St Lucia, you drive on the **left side** of the road.

In and around Castries, Soufrière and Marigot Bay, you can also take advantage of the convenient and fun **water taxi** system, mostly used by tourists and especially handy for getting to nearby beaches.

In addition to the organized sporting activities listed elsewhere in this guide (see Chapter 11), several companies offer unique **tours** of the island, which may be worth considering if time is short.

Buses

Identifiable by an "H" on the licence plate, St Lucia's **buses** are small vans with customized windscreens emblazoned with colourful names such as "Tempt Me" or "Redemption". Though all of the island's buses are privately owned, **fares** are set by the government and are inexpensive: you'll pay no more than EC$8 to travel between any two points on the island. Schedules are less predictable, though, with most drivers waiting until the bus is full before setting off; as a general rule, though, services between major towns run every thirty to sixty minutes from about 6am until 10pm on weekdays, with a reduced timetable on Saturdays; practically no buses run on Sundays. Small cement pavilions serve as **bus stops**, but if you flag a bus down anywhere along a route, it will probably stop if it isn't jammed full.

In **Castries**, all the **bus terminals** and main stops are located in the downtown area. Services **north** to Gros Islet and Cap Estate leave from the Marketing Board lot behind the Castries Central Market. For Vieux Fort and the **south**,

head to the terminal along Jean Baptiste Road, while
Soufrière buses leave from Peynier Street. Anse la Raye
and **Marigot** buses depart from the corner of Chisel and
Victoria streets, and for Morne Fortune from the south section of Louis Street.

In **Vieux Fort**, buses to Castries leave from New Dock
Road on the south side of the airport, while the stand for
west coast buses to Soufrière is also south of the airport at
Clarke Street, next to a traffic light and a Shell service station.

Sample fares

Buses

Castries to: Vieux Fort EC$6, Dennery EC$3, Soufrière EC$8,
Gros Islet EC$2.
Soufrière to: Vieux Fort EC$7.
Vieux Fort to: Dennery EC$3, Gros Islet EC$8.

Taxis

George F.L. Charles Airport to: downtown Castries EC$15,
Rodney Bay EC$35, Cap Estate EC$50, Vieux Fort EC$130.
Downtown Castries to: Soufrière EC$155, Anse la Raye EC$65.
Hewanorra International Airport to: Soufrière EC$130,
downtown Castries EC$125, Gros Islet EC$150.

Taxis

Taxis, whether sedan vehicles or minivans, are identifiable
by an "H" on the licence plate and are in plentiful supply.
You'll see them cruising for fares on the streets or squares of
the main towns, and at obvious locations such as airports,
cruise ship terminals, hotels and tourist spots like Pigeon
Island and Reduit Beach. In terms of price, though, it does-
n't really matter where you start your journey; though all

taxis are unmetered, **fares** are set by the government, and drivers are required to carry a rate sheet in their car. While most drivers stick to the set rates, it's always best to confirm the fare before getting in.

Taxis also offer **guided tours** at a rate of US$20 per hour (for as many as four people), or US$140 for a full day; for each extra person the charge is US$5 per hour. Unlike standard fares, this rate is often negotiable.

Car rental

Car rental **rates** start at US$50 per day for a compact, manual-shift vehicle without air conditioning, and go as high as US$90 for a luxury model. Jeeps and other 4WD vehicles, which you'll need to explore some parts of the island, range from US$65 to US$85. You'll generally pay less during low season, or if you rent for three or more days; discounts of up to 15 percent are also offered throughout the year by some companies if you present one of the coupons available from the tourist board booth at the airports. While mileage is unlimited, rates don't include **petrol**, which at the time of writing costs around EC$6.75 per imperial gallon. Note that you need to be **aged 21** or over to rent a car, and some companies require a minimum age of 25.

Before you get into the rental car, go over it with the attendant to ensure that the spare tyre is in good shape and there is a jack. Note that collision and liability **insurance** will cost as much as US$15 per day; however, certain credit cards allow you to waive the on-site insurance and remain covered as long as you pay for the rental using the card. Call your credit card company to enquire.

Car rental companies

Avis Castries ℂ451-6976, Hewanorra airport ℂ454-6325, George F.L. Charles Airport ℂ452-2046.

Driving in St Lucia

As less than half of St Lucia's 800km of paved roads are on flat land, driving can be a challenge. The **west coast road** from Cap Estate in the north to Vieux Fort in the south has been vastly improved in recent years, but is full of twists and turns, steep hills and, during the rainy season, possible mudslides. Connecting Castries to Vieux Fort via Dennery, the **central** and **east coast highway** is in excellent shape and the quickest way to get from the south to the north of the island. In the **north**, the roads that link the east and west coasts are horrifically potholed at times, and often impassable without a 4WD vehicle. The same goes for roads in the **south** that head up into the central rainforests, which deteriorate the further you head into the interior. Driving in the **towns** is also challenging; all have a surfeit of one-way roads which are clogged with traffic parked on both sides, and traffic jams are always imminent.

Signage is sporadic at best. Major turnoffs are usually marked, but the signs have sometimes faded. Many roads don't have names at all but are known as the "road to Cas-en-Bas" and so on, but you should be able to find your way if armed with a good **road map** (see p.22).

Budget Castries ℂ452-0233, Hewanorra airport ℂ454-5311.
Cool Breeze Soufrière ℂ459-7729, Hewanorra airport ℂ454-7898.
Cost Less Gros Islet ℂ450-3416.
Courtesy Gros Islet ℂ452-8140.
Economy George F.L. Charles Airport ℂ451-7997.
Gibin Rodney Bay ℂ452-9528.
Guy's Gablewoods Mall ℂ451-7147, George F.L. Charles Airport ℂ451-7885.
Hertz Castries ℂ452-0680, Hewanorra airport ℂ54-9636, George F.L. Charles Airport ℂ451-7351.

National Castries ℂ450-8721, Hewanorra airport ℂ454-6699, George F.L. Charles Airport ℂ452-3050.

Motorbike rental

Though it is possible to get around St Lucia on a **motorbike**, it's obviously less safe than a car, and you'll have to watch out for hazards that you might not encounter at home, such as torrential tropical rain, large potholes and animals darting across the roads. You won't have space for much luggage, and wearing a heavy helmet in the heat can be uncomfortable – St Lucian riders rarely use them. Having said that, motorcycles and scooters are certainly less expensive than cars, starting at US$30 per day for bikes in the 250–550cc range – you'll also have to obtain the three-month temporary driver's licence required by all foreigners renting vehicles on the island (see p.28). Wayne's Motorcycle Centre, just north of Castries (ℂ452-2059), is the island's only motorbike **rental outlet**.

Water taxis

Generally small wooden boats that carry no more than four passengers, many of St Lucia's **water taxis** are in fact fishing boats moonlighting for extra cash. In the **Soufrière** area, where a water taxi association acts as a dispatcher (see p.101), boats carry passengers from the town's waterfront to many of the beaches in the area for about EC$25 one way – a quick and fun way to travel. Also on offer are forty-minute sightseeing trips to Castries (EC$300 round-trip for two people); a regular one-way trip to Castries for a minimum of four people costs EC$63 per person. In Castries harbour, water taxis ferry passengers (mainly from the cruise ships) between the Pointe Seraphine shopping complex and the downtown docks.

Tours

Several local companies offer conventional **guided tours** of St Lucia's east coast and central mountains, aboard big, brightly painted and quite obviously tourist-filled 4WD trucks. Most are all-day, all-inclusive expeditions averaging at a mind-numbing US$90 per person, with stops at waterfalls, high-mountain viewing areas and beaches; some involve rainforest hikes of up to three hours. Lunch, refreshments and admission to selected sites are part of the deal, and you are picked up at your hotel. You won't be part of an intimate group, however – some companies set out with as many as forty people. For more information, contact Jungle Tours in Castries (✆450-0434) or Sunlink Jeep Safaris in Rodney Bay (✆452-9678).

A more adventurous option are the inland and coastal **guided walks** offered by the St Lucia National Trust (✆452-5005) and the Forest and Lands Department (✆450-2231 or 2375). The Trust offer walking tours of the Fregate and Maria Islands nature reserves, the arid Pointe Hardy area (see p.93) and the Morne Fortune historic sites (see p.73) for between EC$48 and EC$80 per person, excluding bus travel (up to EC$25). Be warned, however, that these walks are not always available due to staffing and, presumably, budget constraints.

....

Hiking routes in the interior are covered in Chapter Seven.

....

The Forest and Lands Department concentrate on the hiking trails within the interior **forest reserves**, and hiring one of their guides is mandatory if you want to enter certain protected parts of the central rainforest. Popular treks include the Edmund Forest (see p.145) cross-island hike, and the Barre de L'Isle or Des Cartier rainforest trails (see p.142 and 146). You pay a flat EC$25 per person for entry

GETTING AROUND: TOURS

to each trail and for the services of a guide, but again, the Forestry Department isn't a professional tour company: ranger stations at the start of trails are not always staffed, so it's not always easy to find a forestry guide on site.

Lastly, breathtaking but exorbitantly priced **aerial tours** of the island are offered by St Lucia Helicopters (©453-6950) from their base at Pointe Seraphine in Castries. The ten-minute northern excursion passes over the west coast and Pigeon Island, as well as the north Atlantic shore, and costs US$40 per person. A twenty-minute southern tour over Soufrière and the central mountains is US$80, and a thirty-minute jaunt around the entire island runs at US$110 per person.

Costs, money and banks

Like most of the Caribbean, St Lucia isn't an inexpensive place to visit. In restaurants and supermarkets, costs are similar to those in the US or Europe. The cheapest shopping is found at the local fish and vegetable markets or roadside stands set up in just about every town and village.

When it comes to **budgeting**, accommodation is likely to be your major expense. For the large upscale properties, think in terms of at least US$250 per night in high season, and US$120 for smaller hotels. Throw in a rental car for US$50 per day, and you're talking serious money. However, if you stay in guesthouses (US$10–25 per night), limit yourself to travelling by bus and eat at smaller local restaurants, you can happily get by on US$30 per day.

Currency and exchange rates

St Lucia's official currency is the **Eastern Caribbean dollar** (EC$), which is also legal tender in Anguilla, Antigua and Barbuda, Dominica, Grenada, Montserrat, St Kitts and Nevis and St Vincent and the Grenadines. Bills come in denominations of EC$100, EC$50, EC$20, EC$10 and EC$5, and there are 50, 25, 10, 5 and 1 cent coins as well as an EC$1 coin. The EC dollar trades against the US dollar at an official rate of EC$2.68 to US$1 for travellers' cheque exchanges, slightly less for cash conversions. This rate has remained stable for years, and only ever varies by a few cents.

In the case of hotels, car rental, restaurants and practically everything related to tourism, most **prices** in St Lucia are quoted in both EC and US dollars, and occasionally only in the latter. In effect, the **US dollar** serves as the island's unofficial currency, and you can use US bills freely in virtually any transaction, though your change will always be in EC dollars. Note that ATM machines only dispense EC dollars.

In this guide, we have endeavoured to quote prices in EC dollars or US dollars as appropriate (for example, EC$ for bus fares and US$ for airfares). However, be aware that on the street, the most common exchange rate is EC$2.50 to US$1, which goes in the vendor's favour – a taxi fare of EC$25 is equal to US$10, not the US$9.30 you'd calculate using the official exchange rate.

Credit cards and travellers' cheques

Major **credit cards** such as Visa, American Express and MasterCard, are widely accepted for payment (the Discover Card is less recognized), and you can also use them to obtain **cash advances** in banks. The island's Royal Bank of Canada

ATMs accept Cirrus and Plus cards, as well as Visa and MasterCard. Machines are located on William Peter Boulevard in Castries, at the Rodney Bay Marina, and on New Dock Road in Vieux Fort. The Caribbean Banking Corporation ATMs at Micoud Street in downtown Castries and Gablewoods Mall, north of town, take the same cards.

US dollar **travellers' cheques** are accepted by many businesses, but it's wise to always carry some cash with you, as taxi drivers, market stalls and many smaller restaurants or guesthouses won't accept credit cards or travellers' cheques.

Banks and exchange

Banks are found in all major towns on the island, with the majority located in Castries. **Opening hours** are Monday to Thursday from 8am to 3pm, and Friday from 8am to 5pm. The National Commercial Bank exchange bureau at Hewanorra airport in Vieux Fort has extended hours (Mon–Tues 12.30–9pm, Wed 4.30–9pm, Thurs 2–9pm, Fri 12.30–9pm, Sat 2.30–9pm, Sun 1–9pm), and the Royal Bank of Canada branch at the Rodney Bay Marina is open from 8am to noon each Saturday.

Banks always offer the most favourable **exchange rate** – while hotels are more convenient, you'll usually get slightly less for your money.

For details of bank branches in St Lucia, see p.215.

Taxes and tipping

Hotels in St Lucia will almost always add two extra charges to their bills that may not be included in quoted room rates: a ten percent **service charge** and an eight percent government **accommodation tax**. These can bring your bill up an alarming eighteen percent – a hefty addition for a week's stay even at a medium-priced hotel – so it's well worth checking whether taxes are included in the price before you book.

....

Remember that you must pay a EC$40 departure tax when leaving St Lucia by air, and an EC$20 tax if you depart by ferry.

....

Restaurants often add a ten percent **service charge** onto the bill as well. In theory, this is designed to be a tip for waiting staff, but in many cases it never reaches their pockets. To compensate, you could of course leave an extra five percent at a restaurant. Similarly, if you want to be sure your chambermaid gets a tip, leave an extra couple of dollars for each night you've stayed.

Post and phones

All major towns and villages have a **post office**; hours vary slightly, but most are open Monday to Friday between 8am and 4.30pm. Offices outside of large towns usually close at 1pm for an hour's lunch break. The General Post Office on Bridge Street in Castries (①452-5157) is the island's largest and has a philatelic bureau. Sending postcards and packages to the US, Canada or Europe costs less than EC$1, but as they can take up to two weeks to reach their destination, you might want to send urgent items home via the **courier services** which have offices in Castries: FedEx are on Derek Walcott Square (©452-1320), DHL are on Manoel Street (©453-1538), and UPS on Bridge Street (©452-7211). Costs vary according to destination and weight, but you can be assured it will be at least ten times the postal rate.

....
When addressing a letter to St Lucia, include "West Indies" after the name and address.
....

Telephones

St Lucia's **phone system** is reliable. Public phone booths are located all around the island and take either **coins** (EC$1 or EC$0.25) or the **phone cards** available from Cable and Wireless offices (see below), post offices, pharmacies, souvenir stores and convenience shops. Phone cards come in denominations of EC$40, EC$20 and EC$10, plus a US$20 version. **Local calls** cost EC$0.25 for two minutes, double that for long-distance.

....
To call St Lucia from overseas, use your country's international access code (001 in the UK, Ireland and New Zealand, 1 in the US and Canada and 00111 from Australia) followed by area code 758 and the seven-digit number.
....

You can send **faxes** and **telegrams** and make phone calls – at substantially cheaper rates than those offered by hotels – from the Cable and Wireless offices in Castries, Gablewoods Mall and Vieux Fort (all Mon–Fri 8am–6.30pm, Sat 8am–12.30pm). **Internet** access is currently limited to a few hotels.

The media

St Lucia's lively **newspapers** provide the lowdown on local news as well as up-to-date entertainment information. The island's main titles are the *Star*, the *Voice* and the *St Lucia Mirror*, all tabloid size and priced at EC$2. The *Voice* was established in 1885, making it one of the oldest newspapers in the region. The three carry much of the same information, mainly focusing on the local political scene, along with some international news and a big sports section. The entertainment section of the *Voice* is good for local events, while the *Star* tends to be the more complete all-around hard news organ. There's also a regional weekend newspaper, *One Caribbean* (EC$2), serving Grenada, Dominica, St Lucia, and St Vincent. *The Crusader* is a free paper with some news and local events, available at book stores, grocery stores and shops.

You can hear local news and current events listings on St Lucia's several AM and FM **radio** stations, among them Gem Radio (94.5 FM), Radio Caribbean (101.1 FM), Radio St Lucia (97.7 FM, 660 AM), and Radio100 Helen (100.1 FM). Of the lot, Radio St Lucia carries more news and talk, while Gem and Radio100 Helen provide a mix of international and local music.

Medium-priced and upscale hotels generally have access to satellite-fed international cable **television** stations, including HBO and some British and French channels. On channels four and five, the local station **HTS** (Helen Television System) offers news and sports broadcasts, local talk shows and some original programmes.

THE MEDIA |

Safety, harassment and drugs

Generally, St Lucia is a safe place for visitors. The usual pre-cautions for avoiding theft are in order, but the worst that most visitors are likely to encounter is some harassment, though even this is usually confined to areas where tourists congregate in numbers, such as the entrance to Pigeon Island, Soufriére waterfront and Reduit Beach. For women travelling alone, however, harassment can be more of an issue.

Personal safety

Petty **theft** is on the increase and occasional robberies have been reported, so it's wise to employ the common sense practices you follow at home. Don't leave your belongings unattended on the beach – ask someone to watch them while you take a dip; avoid public beaches late at night (the moon might be out, and so might a few thugs); carry your wallet or purse in a pouch or front pocket rather than an open bag; and avoid pulling out large wads of cash when shopping in the street or market. If you've got a rental car, never leave valuables in plain view, and always lock the doors when you leave it. Lastly, it's sensible to check for "H" plates on all vehicles declaring themselves taxis.

If you are unlucky enough to have something stolen or an offence is committed against you, you should contact the

....

**Details of embassies and consulates in St Lucia
are listed on p.216.**

....

local police immediately, and if you want to make an insurance claim, you'll need to get a police report. Local officers are usually friendly and happy to help, though things may take a little longer than you're used to.

Police stations in St Lucia

Castries ℂ452-2372
Choiseul ℂ459-3233
Dennery ℂ453-4277
Gros Islet & Rodney Bay ℂ452-8155
Soufrière ℂ459-7333
Vieux Fort ℂ454-6333

Usually amounting to a few assertive vendors trying to make some money, **harassment** is a subjective problem. In St Lucia, it's nothing like as bad as in other Caribbean destinations, and is unlikely to ruin your trip or inhibit your interaction with St Lucians. However, as a tourist, you will inevitably be approached by people selling carvings, aloe sunburn treatments, T-shirts or hair-braiding services, particularly in heavily visited parts of the island such as Reduit Beach, Castries Central Market, Soufrière waterfront and the streets of Gros Islet during the Friday night party. A firm but respectful "no, thank you" usually works, much like it should.

Emergency numbers

Police ℂ999, **Fire and ambulance** ℂ911,
Victoria Hospital, Castries ℂ452-2421.

POLICE STATIONS, EMERGENCY NUMBERS |

Drugs

Though **drugs** are available, they are of course **illegal** in St Lucia, where the vigorous anti-drugs stance includes occasional sweeps of areas where such substances are known to be handled, such as the Gros Islet street party. **Crack cocaine** and **marijuana** are the most common narcotics, and increasing use by island youths has led to police consternation and crackdowns; officers often work undercover. Always bear in mind that St Lucia is a small island. If you buy drugs, only you and the dealer and about thirty other people will know instantly, and one of them may owe a favour to the local authorities. As a rule, visitors should be extra wary of drug use in St Lucia; prosecutions of foreigners are not unknown, and you do not want to spend time in a St Lucian lock-up.

Women travellers

By and large, **women** travelling to St Lucia alone stand the chance of incurring some harassment or, at the very least, lively interest in their solo status. In the beaches and resort areas, you'll find that some men will circle about like airplanes waiting for permission to land. Most of the time, this is irritating rather than threatening, but there's always a small chance that a situation could turn nasty.

To minimize potential problems, it's important not to cast aside your common sense just because you feel like you're in paradise. Don't contemplate going to the Gros Islet street party on your own, don't sunbathe alone on secluded beaches, head off into the rainforest with a stranger or traipse off to the market in a bikini, and always trust your instincts. Regardless of the cultural backgrounds involved, flirtations are easily assessed; if you think a man is interested, he probably is. Bear in mind that women who've visited

St Lucia before you have set the precedent, and some were actively seeking sexual encounters. If you're not interested, be very clear about it – a firm "no" works most of the time. It's also a good idea to develop a sense of humour concerning the whole business of come-ons; most of it probably has more to do with your perceived economic status than your film-star looks. If you do feel a situation taking a turn for the worse, make a fuss and noise (much like St Lucian women do), and immediately head for a crowd.

Shopping

St Lucia is not brimming with opportunities for **shopping**, although those seeking duty-free items, crafts and art will find plenty to feed their appetites. Most shops **open** on weekdays between 8.30am and 12.30pm, and from 1.30 to 4.30pm, and on Saturdays from 8am to 12.30pm. Shops at Gablewoods Mall, just north of Castries, stay open until 7pm on weekdays and Saturdays; Pointe Seraphine duty-free shops stay open until 2pm on Saturday. Very few shops keep Sunday hours, though you may find some open if there's a cruise ship moored up at Port Castries.

Gablewoods Mall is a good all-round place for some shopping with some thirty shops ranging from chemists to supermarkets to craft shops, as well as bank branches, a post office and several restaurants.

Duty-free shopping

As the island's cruise ship destination, Castries is your best bet for **duty-free** shopping. The **Pointe Seraphine** complex on the north side of the harbour has 25 outlets that stock jewellery, watches, crystal, perfumes, sunglasses, clothing, cigars and electronics as well as stores selling touristy items and souvenirs such as coconut carvings, T-shirts and beach wear. The Sunshine Bookshop here sells paperback novels, newspapers and magazines, plus books with St Lucian themes. Across the harbour from Pointe Seraphine and reachable via a shuttle ferry, the **La Place Carenage** duty-free centre at the North Wharf on Jeremie Street is a smaller branch of Pointe Seraphine.

Although the term "duty-free" implies that the vendor has not paid import duty on its goods and is therefore in a position to pass on its savings to the consumer, this isn't always the case, and you may not always be making a saving. To ensure you get a good deal, it's best to have an idea of what potential purchases would cost at home, and compare prices. Also, don't forget that duty-free items are subject to customs allowances in your own country.

Crafts

Crafts are on sale throughout the island, and browsing around the markets and shops is half the fun of a craft-buying excursion. A wide range of inexpensive carvings, paintings, T-shirts and the like are sold at **Castries'** Central Market and the Vendor's Arcade, downtown on Jeremie and Peynier streets respectively. Prices are good and items range from occasionally tacky carvings or straw baskets to intricate wood sculptures. In **Soufrière**, stop at the Crafts Centre at the north end of the waterfront walkway for an inexpensive and varied selection of souvenirs; also in the southwest, the

Choiseul Arts and Craft Centre (℡459-3226) is the island's premier local outlet. Their pottery, mats, carvings, wicker baskets and traditional wood furniture are high quality and reasonably priced. Bright island-style **clothing**, wraps and beach wear are the hallmarks of Bagshaw Studios (℡452-2139) out on the La Toc Road south of Castries, and of Caribelle Batik (℡452-3785) on the Morne.

Art

St Lucia's **art galleries** include Eudovic's Studio on Morne Fortune (℡452-2747; see p.74), where you can buy original sculptures and watch artisans at work; Artsbit on Brazil Street in Castries (℡452-7865), which displays works by local artists; and local artist Llewellyn Xavier's St Lucia Fine Art at Pointe Seraphine (℡450-9155), which has a large collection of this local artist's oils on canvas and prints.

Markets and supermarkets

Shopping for fresh fruits, vegetables and fish at **local markets** such as the main Central Market in Castries, and the dozens of smaller markets around the island, is the best way to save money and have fun doing it. **Bargaining** is not a blood sport in St Lucia, but you can banter nicely about prices with the vendor, and will often get a better deal; bear in mind, though, that a "heap" of mangoes, for instance, meaning about eight fruits, is EC$1, hardly a price worth sweating over. Shopping at **supermarkets** is another way to save on eating costs, and those listed overleaf have good selections of fresh fruits and vegetables, bakery items, meats and deli fare.

For more on St Lucian food, see pp.174–77.

ART, MARKETS AND SUPERMARKETS

Supermarkets

Julian's Supermarket, Gablewoods Mall, Sunny Acres
(Mon–Thurs 8am–8pm, Fri & Sat 8am–9pm,
Sun 9am–1pm).
Glace Supermarket, Marisule, Castries (Mon–Sat
8am–8pm, Sun 8am–noon).
JQ Supermarket, Bridge St, Castries (Mon–Wed
8am–6pm, Thurs 8am–7pm, Fri 8am–8pm,
Sat 8am–4pm).

Festivals and public holidays

Of St Lucia's roster of **festivals and public holidays**, the
main events are the **St Lucia Jazz Festival**, an internation-
al-class event held at various venues islandwide in May, and
the July **Carnival**, a joyful mishmash of street parades, costume competitions and monumental parties. Unless
otherwise indicated, more information and specific dates for
all events listed in this section can be obtained from the St
Lucia tourist board offices on the island and worldwide; the
tourist board Web site – *slutour@candw.lc* – is also a good
source of information on new events.

Annual events

February

Independence Day on February 22 commemorates the original 1979 ceremony, with political speeches and parades.

May

The **Festival of Comedy** (©452-5005) is the St Lucia National Trust's annual fundraiser and comprises two nights of local comedy acts and theatre at the Cultural Centre in Castries and Pigeon Island. Tourists are welcome, though some plays might be in difficult-to-understand Patois.

The four-day **St Lucia International Jazz Festival** swings into action at the Cultural Centre on the outskirts of Castries, at Pigeon Island and at various spots around the country, including some smaller, more intimate venues in the south (see p.198).

June

The **Feast of St Peter** (also called Fishermen Day) takes place on June 29, and involves religious services and the blessing of fishing boats. It is particularly well attended in Dennery, a mainstay of the industry.

July

Steeped in St Lucia's strong French and Roman Catholic traditions, one of the most popular annual festivities is **Carnival** (see p.200), also known by its Patois name, Jounen Kweyol, and comprising a week of costumed street parades, calypsoing and general partying in the Castries area.

August

Christianity has brought saint's day celebrations to St Lucia, such as La Rose on August 30, also called the **Feast of the**

Rose of Lima. Micoud is a well-known hot-spot for the festivities, but island-wide activities include religious services, flower shows, costume parades, balls, feasts and performances of traditional song and dance.

October

Held in late October, **Jounen Kweyol Entenasyonnal** (International Creole Day) sees Creole-language islands celebrating their language and culture through music, storytelling and dance. In St Lucia, most events take place in Castries.

The **St Lucia Billfishing Tournament** is an opportunity for local and international anglers to compete for big fish and big prizes.

La Marguerite (Feast of St Margaret Mary Alacoque) on October 17 honours the saint with religious services, sports activities and folk performances.

November

November 22, **St Cecilia's Day** (also known as the Feast of Musicians), is celebrated with performances of traditional folk music alongside more modern jazz and calypso.

December

National Day on December 13 is also the **Feast of St Lucy**, marked by island-wide cultural festivals and sports activities such as boat races and football games.

A new entry to St Lucia's events roster is the early-December **St Lucia Country Festival**, four days of twanging banjos in the tropics. Past musicians have included the Charlie Daniels Band, Neal McCoy and the late Tammy Wynette. Events are held at Pigeon Island and the Derek Walcott Theatre at the *Great House* restaurant in Cap Estate.

Public Holidays

January 1	New Year's Day
February 22	Independence Day
March/April	Good Friday & Easter Monday
May 1	Labour Day
Seventh Monday after Easter	Whit Monday
First Monday in August	Emancipation Day
October 25	Thanksgiving Day
November 1	All Soul's Day
December 13	National Day
December 25	Christmas Day
December 26	Boxing Day

THE GUIDE

Castries

ome to some sixty thousand people (more than a third of the island's total population), St Lucia's capital of **CASTRIES**, on the northwest coast, is a metaphor for contemporary West Indian urban culture: at times busy and congested, at times somnolent and peaceful, the town feels somewhat stuck between a centuries-old West Indian lifestyle and a desperate push to modernize. Though Castries is easy to navigate on foot, the town is not particularly blessed with museums, theatres or historical sights, and you'll find that it's primarily a place where people go to conduct business or do some shopping rather than take sightseeing trips.

Overall, Castries has a look of **modernity**; particularly around the waterfront and government complex areas, the town bristles with gleaming, towering structures of glass, concrete and steel, while the classic West Indian look of brightly painted wood and intricate gingerbread fretwork has largely been lost over the years. But that's not the town's fault. Castries burned to the ground in spectacular **conflagrations**, not once, but four times, the last in 1948. Many of the original colonial structures were lost and have been replaced by nondescript, fireproof structures.

Despite its contemporary feel, Castries retains a certain unaffected charm, due more to its setting than anything else. The town is wrapped around the deep harbour of **Port Castries**, where hundreds of cruise ships dock each year to unload credit-card toting tourists for a day of duty-free shopping at the city's malls. This is also where massive cargo ships call to deliver fuel or load up with bananas and other island produce. Spreading back from the harbour is **downtown** Castries, a dozen or so blocks of noisy streets, shops, bus stands and general congestion between Jeremie Street, Chausee Road in the east, Brazil Street in the south and Manoel Street in the southwest. The heart of the area is the bustling **Castries Central Market**, which offers a rich mix of colour, aroma and decibels. At the centre of downtown, there's a bit of greenery at **Derek Walcott Square**, formerly Columbus Square, and scattered throughout the city are several busy open-air vegetable markets, craft markets and shopping centres.

North of downtown and across the harbour, government office-lined John Compton Highway leads toward **Vigie Peninsula**, a flat spit of partially reclaimed land which hosts the island's largest duty-free complex, **Pointe Seraphine**, as well as the small **George F.L. Charles Airport** and several hotels and waterfront restaurants. Castries is surrounded by hills to the east and south: the southern Morne Fortune range once provided a natural defence for the island's various occupiers, and the remains of several forts and batteries are scattered throughout the area (see Chapter Two).

Some history

Though there's little physical trace, Castries is a veritable repository of St Lucia's **history**. In 1651, French settlers built a bastion on the peninsula now called Vigie, on the northern outskirts of the area that would become Castries. The settlement grew over the years, and by 1767 the population had shifted south to the banks of a river that flowed into a deep harbour the French called Petit Cul de Sac. The settlement was renamed in 1785 in honour of the Marquis de Castries, a minister of the French navy and one of the architects of French military efforts in the Caribbean.

The town has flourished as a **port** ever since, despite the successive fires and several disastrous hurricanes – not to mention the minor interruption of the French Revolution, which saw Republicans descend on the island to round up and execute selected members of the French nobility – a guillotine was set up in the Place d'Armes, now Derek Walcott Square.

Castries remained a busy port throughout nineteenth-century British rule, becoming an important **refuelling station** for coal-burning steamships on long ocean voyages, and a convenient stopover for massive cargo and military ships. The port expanded slowly, and new docks and piers were built throughout the twentieth century, some on reclaimed land.

By the early twentieth century, Castries' population had burgeoned, and the streets were packed full of warehouses, homes and shacks – most made of wood and stacked alongside each other like matches in a box. As it turned out, that's exactly the way they behaved. In May 1927, a large **fire** swept through the downtown area, destroying half the city. And in June 1948, another tremendous blaze levelled nearly the entire town. Castries' recovery from these fires was swift, and today the city has settled into a comfortable existence as a mercantile port, tourist destination and seat of government.

Arrival

St Lucia's regional airport lies about a kilometre from downtown Castries, and the city is a logical first destination if you **arrive** by air from another Caribbean island; large, high-speed ferries travelling between neighbouring islands dock in the downtown area. The capital is also a public transport hub: several informal bus depots are scattered around town, where incoming passengers are dropped off, and from where you can catch buses to all areas of the island.

Reviews of accommodation in Castries start on p.154.

By air

Formerly known as Vigie Airport, Castries' small **George F.L. Charles Airport** (℃452-2893) on Vigie Peninsula mostly handles small aircraft arriving from neighbouring Caribbean islands and South America. Several **regional airlines** are based here, including HelenAir, St Lucia's national carrier. There's a **tourist information** booth (℃452-2596) immediately outside the arrival doors, open daily for all incoming flights, as well as the small *La Vigie restaurant* and a row of **car rental** kiosks. Just outside the arrival area is a **taxi** stand (℃452-1599); the five-minute taxi ride to downtown costs EC$15.

For more information on regional airlines and flights to and from St Lucia, see pp.17–18.

By sea

Some 300 cruise ships – and more than 300,000 passengers – stop off at St Lucia each year, and most of them dock at the north side of Castries harbour, conveniently close to the Pointe Seraphine duty-free shopping complex (see p.64). At the back of the complex, a signposted jetty is the place to catch a **water taxi** for the five-minute ride to the North Wharf – also called the La Place Carenage Wharf – on Jeremie Street in downtown Castries (US$1). Boats cross the harbour every 30 to 45 minutes, more frequently when there's a cruise ship at the Pointe Seraphine dock.

If you've arrived from Guadeloupe, Dominica or Martinique via the high-speed **L'Express des Iles** ferry (see p.19), you'll disembark at the North Wharf docks, from where it's a short walk southeast along Jeremie Street to buses, taxis and the rest of town.

By road

If you arrive in Castries by **bus**, you'll be dropped off at one of several locations, including the Marketing Board, Jeremie Street, Darling Road, Peynier Street and Manoel Street. These are all downtown stops within walking distance of each other, close to taxis and other forms of city transport.

For more on bus services from the capital, see p.28.

Castries is not an easy city to navigate by **car**. On weekdays in particular, the narrow streets are congested and so choked with randomly parked cars and trucks that it's extremely difficult to find a space for your own vehicle. If you're lucky, you might find a place at the **car park** outside the Marketing Board building behind the market on Jeremie Street, but it's best to park on the city outskirts (Pointe Seraphine is a good bet), and take a taxi or water taxi to downtown Castries.

Information

The administrative office of the **St Lucia Tourist Board** is on the second floor of the Pointe Seraphine complex (℃452-4094 or 452-5968, fax 453-1121). However, visitors are better served by the knowledgeable and helpful staff of the **tourist information kiosk** downstairs (Nov–April Mon–Fri 9am–5pm, Sat 9am–2pm; May–Oct Mon–Fri 9am–4pm, Sat 9am–2pm; ℃452-7577), which often remains open to accommodate cruise ship visitors who arrive outside regular opening hours. The kiosk stocks free maps, brochures and information about Castries and the rest of the island. George F.L. Charles Airport also has a kiosk where you can get the same free maps and brochures as well as general information, and there's another kiosk near the La Place Carenage docks on Jeremie Street, opening mainly for cruise ship traffic.

Downtown Castries

The focal point of downtown Castries, **Derek Walcott Square** is the perfect place to rest after a hard day's sightseeing. Lining the square to the south, **Brazil Street**'s handful of classic West Indian wooden buildings make an overly elegant backdrop to the constant stream of pedestrians and traffic, while to the east, the imposing **Cathedral of the Immaculate Conception** towers over the grass, the St Lucian showpiece of the Roman Catholic Church. To the north of the square, vendors at the frenetic **Castries Central Market** hawk everything from fruit to cooked lunches.

DEREK WALCOTT SQUARE

Map 2, D6–E6.

Though it's a peaceful place today, **Derek Walcott Square** has had a turbulent history. In the late eighteenth century following the French Revolution, the square was known as the Place d'Armes, and a **guillotine** was set up by Republicans anxious to do away with selected members of the nobility. It was then labelled Promenade

Square, and later still Columbus Square (1892), before being renamed in 1993 after the St Lucia Nobel Prize-winning poet and playwright. Bordered by Brazil, Micoud, Bourbon and Laborie streets, this small city centrepiece is a grassy and landscaped oasis in an otherwise congested town. The east side of the square is shaded by an immense saman tree, thought to be more than 400 years old. Samans are also known as **rain trees** – their leaves are so thick and plentiful that after a downpour, the tree continues to "rain" for a time. The small gazebo adjacent to the tree is used for band concerts and public gatherings. A **memorial** and plaque dedicated to native St Lucians who died during the great world wars occupies the west end of the park, and benches and resting spots are scattered around, favoured by office workers catching a quick lunch in the shade.

Though they now house banks, gift shops, restaurants and the Cathedral of the Immaculate Conception (see p.61), the busy streets bordering Derek Walcott Square are the oldest, and most attractive, parts of the capital; from here, Castries' other sights radiate out in a discernible pattern.

BRAZIL STREET

Map 2, D6–F6.

Bordering the south side of Derek Walcott Square, **Brazil Street** is the city's congested and busy architectural showcase. Miraculously, many of its structures escaped the hurricanes and fires of the early colonial days and the mid-twentieth century. Excellent examples of colonial West Indian architecture stand toward the centre of the street, directly across from Derek Walcott Square. A white Victorian town house with green trim festooned by white gingerbread fretwork, the restaurant now called *Rain* dates

Derek Walcott

Born on St Lucia in 1930, poet and playwright **Derek Walcott** was awarded the Nobel Prize in Literature in 1992. He remains one of the finest writers, Caribbean or otherwise, of recent times, a fervent proponent of the West Indian cultural and linguistic rhythms he employs and celebrates in his writing.

Walcott was educated at St Mary's College in Castries and at the University of the West Indies in Jamaica, and his poetry was first published when he was just 18 and still a student. He attended acting school when he moved to New York in the late 1950s, and in 1959, he established the **Trinidad Theatre Workshop** in Port of Spain, and continued to publish poems and plays throughout the 1960s. His first collection of poetry, *Another Life* (1973), established him as a significant writer. Among more than 45 major works are the play *Dream on Monkey Mountain* (1970) and the 1990 epic *Omeros*, a broad narrative that mixes Homeric legend with West Indian themes. More recently, he collaborated with singer Paul Simon in the Broadway musical *The Capeman*.

Walcott's ethnic origins are British, Dutch and African; his culture is French and British with an American twist; and his sensibility is wholly West Indian. In awarding Walcott the 1992 prize, the Nobel academy commented that "In him, West Indian culture has found its great poet", and called his work "a poetic oeuvre of great luminosity, sustained by a historical vision, the outcome of a multicultural achievement". Today, Derek Walcott divides his time between homes in St Lucia and in the United States, where he is a professor of English at Boston University.

DEREK WALCOTT

back to 1885, and is one of the city's best-preserved structures. Next door are two equally ornate buildings of the same period, also sporting the gingerbread motif and now private residences and shops, while a few hundred feet east is the brightly coloured *Creole House* restaurant, with its second-storey verandah decked out with intricate fretwork.

CATHEDRAL OF THE IMMACULATE CONCEPTION

Map 2, E6. Services Sat 7.30pm, Sun 6am & 7.30am, Children's Mass Sun 10.30am. Donations accepted ✆452-2271.

Nearly ninety percent of St Lucians are **Roman Catholic** – a legacy of years of French colonial rule – and the cornerstone of the island's faith is the imposing brick-and-mortar **Cathedral of the Immaculate Conception** on Laborie and Micoud streets, which seats two thousand communicants. Dominating the east side of Derek Walcott Square, the cathedral site has been occupied by various churches as far back as the early eighteenth century, all of which were destroyed by successive fires and storms. The foundation of the current structure dates to 1894, but today's building was not completed until 1931. In 1957, the former church was granted the status of a cathedral, and was visited by **Pope John Paul II** when he toured the Caribbean in 1986.

Unless Mass is in progress, you're allowed inside to have a look around the ornate **interior**, bathed in rich red and diffused yellow light from ceiling portals, and busy with detailed carved wood inlay, wood benches, iron ceiling supports and stately pillars. Depicting black saints and the work of the Catholic Church in St Lucia, the **wall murals** are by well-known local artist **Dunstan St Omer**, who painted them in 1985 prior to the pope's visit. Note the ceiling paintings of Catholic saints and apostles, with Saint Lucie in the centre.

CATHEDRAL OF THE IMMACULATE CONCEPTION |

CENTRAL MARKET TO LA PLACE CARENAGE

Map 2, E4–D4.

Vividly colourful and often loud, **Central Market** on Jeremie Street at the northern perimeter of downtown is one of the busiest parts of Castries. Newly built and rambling, the structure houses several markets, all of which are busiest on Saturday mornings. Inside are rows of **craft booths**, with vendors selling baskets, spices, carvings, T-shirts, straw hats and tacky souvenirs. The prices here are about as good as they get, and certainly better than at Pointe Seraphine, but do tend to increase a little if a cruise ship is in town. In the centre of the craft section is a non-functioning cement **fountain** resplendent with protruding lion heads painted bright red; a sign above implores: "No Smoking, No Spitting." The fountain is the most obvious remnant of the original market, built in 1894; you can still see parts of the old iron structure in the ceiling and walls.

Under an orange roof to the left of the Jeremie Street entrance is the colourful and busy **fruit and vegetable market**, where you can find a wealth of fresh produce: mangoes, sugar cane, soursop, ginger, bananas, plantains and earth-encrusted tubers of yam and dasheen are piled on cardboard boxes or makeshift stands of wood. Good deals can be had here, for instance a "heap" of mangoes (about seven or eight) for around EC$1. Some vendors also put out their stalls in the open air at the back of the market.

Also at the market's back end, on the north side, an alleyway of fifteen or so small, steam- and smoke-belching **restaurant** stalls (see p.178) fill the air with tempting aromas. Inexpensive and reliable, these are possibly the best places to eat in town, serving up huge portions of seafood, rotis, rice and beans, or meat and dumpling dishes at plastic tables jammed into the narrow corridor between the stalls. At the end of the restaurant arcade, **Lewis Street** is also lined with shops and vendors selling vegetables, fruit and crafts.

Across from the Central Market on **Peynier Street**, and easily identifiable by the rust-coloured roof, is the **Vendor's Arcade**, another set of craft stalls selling the same rather tacky wares at slightly higher prices.

Heading west from the Central Market along Jeremie Street, with the harbour on your right, the **La Place Carenage** duty-free shopping centre is five minutes' walk away. Though not as large as the mall at Pointe Seraphine, the centre has several craft and vegetable stalls, art galleries and boutiques. You'll find some good deals here, without the trouble of travelling over the water to Pointe Seraphine. La Place Carenage shops are generally open weekdays from 9am to 5pm, Saturday from 9am to 2pm, and, if cruise ships are visiting, on Sunday from 9am to 4pm.

Vigie Peninsula

Framing the northern half of Port Castries, the heavily developed **Vigie Peninsula** is partially made up of land recovered from the sea by successive government reclamation projects. At the south of the peninsula, and overlooking the bay, are the **Pointe Seraphine shopping complex** and two **cruise ship berths**, while government offices converted from eighteenth- and nineteenth-century military buildings are clustered around the sparsely developed western tip; a lighthouse overlooks the ocean here, but it's not open to visitors. Running semi-diagonally through the centre of the peninsula is the **George F.L. Charles Airport**, and parallel to the runway is the expansive **Vigie Beach**, where there's a waterfront hotel and several excellent seafood restaurants.

CHAPTER ONE

POINTE SERAPHINE

Map 2, B2. Nov–April Mon–Fri 9am–5pm, Sat 9am–2pm;
May–Oct Mon–Fri 9am–4pm, Sat 9am–2pm.

Outside the usual Caribbean tourist paraphernalia and
comestibles, Castries is not a shopper's paradise. However,
at the north end of the inner harbour, a small centre of
consumerism exists in the form of the **Pointe Seraphine**
duty-free complex. Built in the early 1990s on reclaimed
land, Pointe Seraphine advertises itself as the Caribbean's
biggest duty-free shopping complex. It's not (the honour
goes to the Charlotte Amalie mall in the US Virgin
Islands), but it is certainly the largest that St Lucia has to
offer, and it's still growing. Two adjacent cruise ship berths
deliver disembarking tourists directly to the stores, while
the **taxi stand** (✆452-1733) and the **water taxi** to downtown Castries (every 30–45min, more frequent when
cruise ships are docked; US$1) stand by to cater for the
day-trippers.

For more on Pointe Seraphine shopping, see p.44.

The twenty-plus **shops** include international chain
stores, as well as local retailers dealing in leather goods,
cigars, music, souvenirs and art. You'll also find a branch
of the National Commercial Bank and the Sunshine
Bookshop here – the latter stocks a selection of British
and US newspapers, including *The Times*, *Miami Herald*
and the *New York Times*, usually a day or two old, as well
as local papers. Outside the **tourist office** on the complex's second floor (see p.21) is the *Ti Café* coffee shop,
serving cappuccino, espresso, juices and other concoctions, a good spot to relax after trekking around the
shops.

POINTE SERAPHINE

64

ALONG PENINSULAR ROAD

Map 3, A5–D5.

Sandwiched between the airport runway and the sea, **Peninsular Road** runs east to west along the length of Vigie Peninsula. To get on to it, take the John Compton Highway north from town, turn right on the Castries-Gros Islet Highway, left at the end of the airport and left again onto the Peninsular Road. Just before you reach the airstrip, the **Choc Bay Cemetery** is on the right, typical of those in the region with its ornately decorated raised white tombs. Forty simple white memorial stones standing in sentry around a large white cross designate the **War Cemetery** section, dedicated to local sailors who were killed in March 1942, when a German submarine skulked into Castries harbour and torpedoed two British ships.

Just west of the cemetery, Peninsular Road flanks the two-kilometre **Vigie Beach**; long and smooth, but with litter-strewn, Duluth brown-grey sand, it's not much to look at, but the water is usually calm and inviting. A few snack vendors are parked here and there, a handful of benches and picnic tables overlook the water, and there's plenty of shade from trees, but for better places to swim and sun yourself, head north to Reduit or south toward Marigot (see p.82 and p.96).

Once clear of the airport, Peninsular Road winds uphill. The entire peninsula was once a fortification, and many of the buildings at the top of the hill are restored military quarters, built from red brick in the late nineteenth century. At the western end of the peninsula, St Lucia's **National Archives** (Mon–Thurs 8.30am–4.30pm, Fri 8.30am–2pm; ©453-1405) are housed in a circa-1890 building: inside, you can browse through hundreds of old photos, lithographs, postcards and maps, which provide a good historical perspective of the island. Also ensconced in an ex-military

65

building adjacent to the archives are the offices of the **St Lucia National Trust** (✆452-5005), where you can obtain brochures and information pamphlets about nature reserves such as the Fregate and Maria islands. A society that seeks to preserve historical sites and other places of national interest, the National Trust has proposed that the entire peninsula be designated a protected site, with the island's first national museum located among the barracks; however, the plans are unlikely to be realized in the foreseeable future.

Around Castries

With beaches, forts and forest-smothered hills, the area **around Castries** is well worth exploring. Even without a car, it's easy to get to all the sights thanks to the capital's good public transport links.

Past the Vigie Peninsula, which encloses the capital to the north, **Choc Bay**'s enviable stretch of golden sand and lively beach bars make a great place to get away from the city heat; just offshore, the tiny **Rat Island** has long shrugged off its former role as a quarantine station, and has been earmarked by Nobel Prize-winner Derek Walcott as a possible site for an artists' colony. Inland from Choc Bay, a smooth, wide road heads toward **Babonneau**, a typical inland village which was home to several vast sugar plantations during the eighteenth century. Also in the interior but to the east of downtown Castries, the **Folk Research Centre** provides a fascinating and unique insight into St Lucian traditions.

Though the capital provides tempting views of far-flung peaks such as the Pitons at Soufrière (see p.107) and of Morne Gimie in the southern interior, the hills that surround the capital allow you to take in the city and much of the north coast; on clear days you can see the island of Martinique, some 40km to the north. West of town the British-built **La Toc Battery** is one of the island's best-preserved stockades, while the historically significant **Morne**

Fortune hills to the south of the city are riddled with remnants of French forts dating back to the eighteenth and nineteenth centuries. Snaking through Morne Fortune's southern foothills, the coastal highway swings down into the verdant and beautiful **Cul de Sac Valley**, noted for its extensive banana fields and for the jarringly unpleasant Hess Oil plant.

Reviews of accommodation around Castries start on p.154.

CHOC BAY

Map 1, E3.

Heading north from Castries, the busy Castries–Gros Islet Highway passes the Vigie Peninsula to the left, while a string of industrial sites, shops, restaurants, hotels and schools lines each side. It's not the most appealing drive on the island, but five minutes out of town and past the peninsula, the highway swings back to the coast and runs parallel to the sweeping two-kilometre **Choc Bay**, fringed to the north by Labrellotte Point, a compact, sheltered bay hosting a couple of luxury resorts, and to the south by **Vide Bouteille Point**, a small promontory which separates Choc and Vigie bays and was the site of St Lucia's first **fort**, built in 1660 by the French – there's nothing left of it today.

From the highway, you'll catch tempting glimpses of the hidden **coves** and honey sand **beaches** that pepper Choc Bay, some of which are lined by hotels (see p.155). The beaches are accessible via several turnoffs, but one of the best places to spend a day is the stretch adjacent to *Waves* (©451-3000), a lively beach bar and restaurant with good food, occasional evening entertainment and an affiliated watersports concession from which you can rent Sunfish sailing boats and windsurfing boards by the hour (around EC$30), as well as beach chairs for US$2 per day. Equally pleasant is the stretch of sand in front of *D's Restaurant*, at the *Edgewater Beach Club* hotel, where you can grab some lunch before heading to the water.

Rat Island

Map 3, E3.

A diminutive cay scattered with scrubby trees and dilapidated buildings, **Rat Island** lies a few hundred yards off the coast at the southern end of Choc Bay. Though currently uninhabited, the island has been occupied in the past – periodic finds of Arawak pottery suggest that Amerindians once settled here, and the cay was also put to use as a **quarantine station** for afflictions such as scarlet fever and smallpox, before being abandoned in the late nineteenth century when infection levels dropped.

Rat Island is notable today for its connection with St Lucia's Nobel Prize-winner **Derek Walcott** (see p.60), who, in conjunction with the government of St Lucia, private donors and grants from Boston University, has proposed the island be redeveloped as an **artists' retreat** so that its "extraordinary solitude" can be fully utilized. The plans include several cottages, as well as a dock, jetty and an amphitheatre, and the intention is to attract artists, writers and actors, both known and unknown, from St Lucia and from further afield. However, though the project has proved to be slow-moving, the plans are expected to be formalized and underway within a few years.

BABONNEAU

Map 1, F4.

About 3km north of the capital at the southern end of Choc Bay, the Castries–Gros Islet Highway swings into the suburban **Sunny Acres** area. On the inland side of the road is **Gablewoods Mall**, one of the island's larger shopping complexes and the place to go if you need to visit a pharmacy or buy groceries. Just past the mall, the winding but un-potholed **Allan Bousquet Highway** strikes into the interior – ten minutes' drive from the coast is the village of **BABONNEAU**, a small farming community huddled into the central hills of the island's northern half, and worth visiting for the sweeping hill views and for a taste of rural St Lucia. Several rivers flow through the hills around the settlement, and some people believe that the town's name is a Patois version of the old French phrase *barre bon eau*, for, roughly, "mountain ridge, good water".

The Allan Bousquet Highway is the easiest route to the attractions of the northeast coast, including the turtle watch at Grande Anse beach.

Babonneau was settled early on in St Lucia's history by Joseph Tascher de la Pagerie, who owned an estate at nearby Paix Bouche and fathered Marie-Joseph Tascher de la Pagerie, better known as **Empress Josephine** of France, wife of Napoleon Bonaparte (see opposite). However, despite the historical infamy, there's not a great deal to see in Babonneau other than a large and vividly coloured **Catholic church** on a hill in the sparsely populated "centre" of the village, which dates back to 1947.

A few kilometres further inland from Babonneau is the Union Nature Trail centre, an agricultural station, mini zoo and hiking trail maintained by the Department of Forest and Lands (see p.33).

FOLK RESEARCH CENTRE

Map 3, D6. Mon–Fri 8.30am–4.30pm; donations accepted.
Morne Pleasant ✆452-2279.

Empress Josephine

St Lucians popularly believe that the girl who would become **Empress Josephine**, wife of Napoleon Bonaparte, came into the world at a plantation estate called Paix Bouche, near **Babonneau**. However, many in neighbouring Martinique claim that she was born on their island, and Josephine's birth records remain a hotly disputed matter of St Lucian national pride. As no birth certificates exist, and the various claims have been supported only by the memories of priests ministering in the late eighteenth century, proof is more a matter of legend than fact. St Lucians will grudgingly acknowledge that Josephine was conceived in Martinique, born in St Lucia and lived here for seven years, before returning to Martinique with her family.

Born Marie-Joseph Tascher de la Pagerie in 1763, Josephine was the daughter of estate owner Joseph Tascher de la Pagerie. In 1779, at the age of sixteen, she married French military officer and nobleman Alexandre, vicomte de Beauharnais. Due to his status as a nobleman, Beauharnais was one of many singled out during the French Revolution's reign of terror, and was **beheaded** in 1794. Josephine married **Napoleon** in 1796, and became empress when the megalomaniacal leader declared himself emperor in 1804. The marriage was short-lived – Napoleon divorced her in 1809, and she died in 1814.

Josephine had two children with Beauharnais, Eugène and Hortense. Keeping things in the family, Hortense later married Napoleon's brother Louis – in essence, Napoleon's step-daughter became his sister-in-law – and bore him a son, the future empire leader Napoleon III.

Set high in the hills east of Castries at Morne Pleasant, the **Folk Research Centre** (or *Plas Wichès Foklò*, to give it its Patois name) is a museum and cultural centre set in an old estate house originally owned by the eminent Deveaux family. Inside is a small and somewhat jumbled **museum**: exhibits include a reproduction of a traditional *ti-kay* hut, and examples of indigenous musical instruments such as the *chak-chak* (condiment tins taped together and filled with seeds), the *banjo bwa payé* (a small banjo), and a *tambou* (a wooden drum with a goatskin head). Also on display are clay pots and a fantasy diorama depicting an ancient St Lucian legend of a witch doctor stepping through a magic door. The small **research library** upstairs holds one of the island's best collections of books, research papers and photographs relating to St Lucia's folklore and history. You can view the collection during opening hours, and librarians are on hand to assist you.

Since it was established in 1973, the centre has spearheaded the movement to preserve and promote St Lucia's heritage, and is especially active during **Carnival**. During the festival, you can call in for a schedule of plays, musical performances and special events based around the celebrations, which take place here and throughout the island. The centre also run a programme of lectures within local schools, as well as staging performances by the in-house **Popular Theatre** group, also known by their Patois name *Teyat Pep La*; for more on their productions, see p.201.

To get to the centre, turn off the Castries–Gros Islet Highway along the L'Anse Road, which strikes inland just south of the airport; you turn off again at the sign for Morne Pleasant.

For more on St Lucia's carnival, see p.200.

LA TOC BATTERY

Map 3, A7. Dec–April Mon–Fri 8.30am–3pm, weekends by appointment; May–Nov by appointment only; EC$6. ℂ451-6300 or 452-7921.

FOLK RESEARCH CENTRE

From downtown Castries, La Toc Road leads west along the south side of the harbour. Toward the western outskirts of town, as the road begins to climb, is the sizeable **Victoria Hospital**, the island's largest; a mile or so beyond, still on La Toc Road, is **La Toc Battery**, one of the island's best-preserved examples of British military bastions. The 2.5-acre, nineteenth-century cement fortification features mounted cannons and dim underground bunkers, tunnels and cartridge storage rooms; one of the bunkers holds a large exhibit of antique bottles. Also in the grounds is a small **botanical garden**, where guides will answer questions and conduct tours at no extra cost.

MORNE FORTUNE

Map 3, B8–C8.

In order to pass from Castries to the south of the island, winding through the loosely demarcated suburb of **Morne Fortune** is inevitable. Comprising a series of hills which flank the capital to the south, the area's high elevation provides striking views of the city, the Vigie Peninsula and the north coast – on a clear day you can see the island of Martinique – and to the south, glimpses of the conical Pitons at Soufrière. The area is reachable via Manoel Street in downtown Castries, which becomes Government House Road as it begins its snakelike ascent.

The main attraction of the Morne Fortune hills are the eighteenth- and nineteenth-century military installations of Fort Charlotte, most still standing and now forming part of an educational and government administrative complex. Parts of the old fort complex are open to the public, while others await restoration.

Also scattered throughout Morne Fortune are several excellent **restaurants**, great places for lunch with panoramic

LA TOC BATTERY, MORNE FORTUNE

views of the harbour below. While you're in the area, it's also well worth checking out **Eudovic's Studio** (©452-2747) on the southern flanks of the hills, where you can watch local **wood carvers** create some extraordinary works under the watchful eye of master artisan Vincent Joseph Eudovic. One of the island's most renowned carvers, Eudovic studied in Africa and works in mahogany, teak and cedar to produce abstract, graceful and flowing pieces. He also uses the local wood **laurier canelle**, now thought to be extinct, but found as stumps and buried roots in the rainforests.

Government House

Map 3, B7.

Unsurprisingly, the focal point of Government House Road is the official residence of the governor general, **Government House**, a regal and looming example of sedate Victorian architecture set some 5km from Castries. Though the house is closed to the public, it's worth heading up for the panoramic outlook over Port Castries, Choc Bay and Labrellotte Point that unravels from a **viewing platform** set just below the house – if you can see past the throngs of craft and snack vendors, that is.

Fort Charlotte

Map 3, B8–C8.

A few winds and turns beyond Government House, Morne Road takes you into the heart of **Morne Fortune** and to the top of the 260-metre Morne Fortune itself, named "Good Luck Hill" by the French. The hills were first fortified by the French in 1768, then recaptured (and renamed **Fort Charlotte**) by the British in 1803. A great battle was fought here in 1796 – a monument on the grounds of Arthur Lewis College (see below) honours the victorious

Royal Inniskilling Fusiliers, who fought for several days on the steep slopes to take the position from the French.

Several of the existing military encampments, cemeteries, barracks and batteries are slated to be restored and opened to the public; however, the process is incomplete and many are still in a state of disrepair. Among those that have received some attention is the **Apostles' Battery**, just off the road south of Government House. Built in 1888-90, it's so named for its four mounted ten-inch guns, but the expansive views from here are probably more eyecatching than the ruin itself. Back on the road and a few hundred metres to the east is **Provost's Redout**, another gun battery built in 1782, also with gorgeous views to the northwest coast. Other sites, not yet refurbished, include the nineteenth-century Old English Cemetery, the old prison cells, guard room and stables.

The best-preserved remnants of the fort are now part of a multipurpose government complex that encompasses offices of the Agricultural Department, the Caribbean Environmental Health Institute and the Organization of Eastern Caribbean States, as well as the **Sir Arthur Lewis Community College**, named after the St Lucian Nobel Prize-winner who is buried in the grounds (see box, p.60). The college itself comprises several larger, nineteenth-century yellow-brick structures with gleaming white columns, all of military origin, which include the Combermere Barracks, a series of three buildings named after Lord Combermere, the commander of British forces in St Lucia between 1817 and 1820. Featuring thick walls, second-floor balconies and archways framing entrance portals, the college's buildings were restored in the late 1960s and look surprisingly modern due to careful refurbishment and ongoing upkeep. You're free to amble about and visit the buildings and Inniskilling monument, which is on the south side of the college complex behind the Combermere Barracks.

FORT CHARLOTTE

Sir Arthur Lewis

Of the three Nobel laureates born on West Indian soil, St Lucia has the honour of claiming two as native sons: Derek Walcott, who won the literature prize in 1992 (see p.60), and **Sir Arthur Lewis**, who was actually born on Antigua in 1915, but emigrated to St Lucia with his family at the age of three. After completing his secondary education at 14, he won a scholarship to study in England. Lewis originally intended to study engineering, but gave up the idea when he realized that, given the tenor of the times, firms were not hiring black engineers. He eventually studied commerce and accounting at the London School of Economics and went on to earn a PhD in Industrial Economics.

Lewis became a professor of economics at the University of Manchester in England, and, in 1963, the year he was knighted for extraordinary service to the realm, he earned a full professorship at Princeton University in New Jersey. Lewis's 1954 book, *The Theory of Economic Growth*, is still regarded as a seminal work in the field of world economic history, and he was also an economic advisor to the United Nations and played an important role in establishing the Caribbean Development Bank in the early 1970s. Shared with American Theodore Schultz, Lewis's Nobel Prize for Economics came in 1979. He died in 1991 at age 76, and is buried at a private plot on the grounds of the Sir Arthur Lewis Community College on Morne Fortune (see p.75).

CUL DE SAC VALLEY

Map 1, D5.

Heading south over the Morne Fortune hills, the immense **Cul de Sac Valley** swings into view as the Castries–Soufrière highway begins to descend. Chiselled out by the Cul de Sac River, one of the island's longest, the valley's relatively flat and extremely fertile plains make it ideal for **farming**, and the area is abundant with banana fields and small holdings. The only blight on the land is a large, modern **Hess Oil plant** and its massive shipping docks, as well as the large main plant of the island's electricity company, Lucelec. Just past Lucelec is the east-bound turnoff for Dennery and the Department of Forest and Lands' Barre de L'Isle Trail (see p.142). The road to Dennery is in great shape, and you can get to the east coast town in twenty minutes or so (see p.131).

South of the valley, the main road heads toward Marigot Bay and, ultimately, Soufrière and the south coast, covered in Chapter Four.

Gros Islet and the north

I n accordance with French administrative divisions that split the island into eleven *quartiers*, St Lucia's compact northern tip is still referred to as the **Quarter of Gros Islet**. The area encompasses the "Golden Mile" resort towns of the northwest coast as well as the remote and arid northern shoreline between Pointe du Cap and Pointe Hardy, and quiet Cas-en-Bas on the rugged northeast coast.

On the west coast, the sweeping, three-kilometre horseshoe of Rodney Bay contains the majority of the Quarter's tourist trappings. **Rodney Bay** town is the most popular resort area, with a deep-water yacht harbour and a sophisticated marina complex packed with shops and restaurants, as well as the superlative, hotel-lined **Reduit Beach**, one of St Lucia's most popular strips of sand with excellent possibilities for watersports. Across the harbour channel is the quiet fishing village of **Gros Islet**, a place to soak up some local flavour at small, unpretentious Creole restaurants. Just about the entire village is overtaken each Friday night for the raucous **street party**, when the streets are blocked off and revellers pour in for a night of music and mingling.

Vendors set up barbecue booths, bars open their doors and loud music is pumped from fat speakers as the crowd gyrates to thumping soca and reggae. It's a big, boisterous party, with a largely congenial crowd of tourists and young St Lucians, all out for a night of dancing and noshing barbecued chicken and fried fish. Gros Islet's beach isn't one of the northwest's best, but on the opposite coastline, **Cas-en-Bas** boasts several secluded places to swim, reachable via rough dirt tracks off the highway.

Rodney Bay's northern half is framed by the heavily visited **Pigeon Island National Historic Park**, a misleadingly named outcrop that was attached to the mainland by a causeway in the 1970s. Heavily fortified by the British in the eighteenth century, the island has now been transformed into a recreation park enjoyed by visitors and St Lucians alike, who come to tour the restored remains of military buildings or enjoy the string of beaches and walking trails. The park also plays the part of performance venue, hosting comedy shows and the headline concerts of the **St Lucia Jazz Festival**.

Despite all the development along the northwest coast, the north does not necessarily feel crowded. Many of the lodgings are secreted away along the shoreline itself, and though the Castries-Gros Islet Highway is thick with cars, buses and taxis on the outskirts of the capital, both the traffic and the tourist buzz thin out north of Pigeon Island, as the road meanders toward hilly **Cap Estate**. Here, the Quarter takes on a more natural feel: calm Caribbean coastline is replaced by cliffs and choppy waters, and the parched peaks provide marvellous views of both the northern coastline and the island of Martinique. A couple of exclusive resorts occupy the coast, while the eastern hills around **Saline Point** and **Pointe Du Cap** (St Lucia's most northerly extremity) are scattered with the palatial homes and villas of the island's elite.

Though St Lucia's northern tip is a slim 8km from the east coast to the west in some parts, travelling over the dirt roads that traverse the area is not an easy proposition, particularly after rains, when a 4WD is recommended. The rough roads to the east coast from Saline Point pass the hardy vegetation of cacti and acacia which indicate the aridity of the region. Rarely visited by tourists, **Pointe Hardy** juts out into the Atlantic at the island's northeast tip, and provides stunning panoramas of the rocky coast, cliffs and crashing surf.

Some history

Artefacts have been found both around Gros Islet and on Pigeon Island, evidence of Carib – and possibly Arawak – settlement dating back 1500 years. However, the earliest written reference to the area is contained in a French map of 1717, which labelled the spot "Le Gros Islet" or "Large Island" for the offshore cay now known as Pigeon Island. This small spit of land gained further notability in 1782, when Britain's Admiral George Rodney established a **fort** there which he used as a base to engage the French (see p.84). Less than ten years later, the area briefly became La Revolution, renamed by the post-Revolutionary French alongside every other St Lucian settlement. When the British regained control of St Lucia later in the century, the name reverted to Gros Islet, and surrounding sugar plantations such as Bonne Terre and Marisule provided some prosperity.

For more on St Lucia's history, see p.221.

At the turn of the twentieth century, Gros Islet itself was little more than a bucolic fishing village bordered by a great marsh. However, during World War II, Allied forces constructed **naval airfields** at Gros Islet (and at Vieux Fort) for the defence of the Panama Canal and the interests of the United States against the German U-boats and other vessels of war that skulked in the area. The naval engineers' attempts to fill in the large mangrove swamp south of the village met, time after time, with failure. At the end of the war, the bases were dismantled and gradually crumbled, but the idea of creating an **inner harbour** to the naturally deep Rodney Bay had taken hold. In 1970, the government dredged the mangrove swamp and let it fill – the ensuing deep-water harbour is now home to one of the island's largest marinas – using sand and sludge removed from the swamp to construct the Pigeon Island causeway.

Inevitably, though, damage has been done. The swamp was once a prime breeding and feeding area for hundreds of species of migrating birds and marine life, such as cattle egrets, herons, the St Lucia black finch and oriole as well as prawns, spiny lobster and conch, most of which have now moved elsewhere. The jury remains out regarding the deeper **environmental issues** – the natural filtration systems provided by the swamp are gone, and ocean currents that flowed around Pigeon Island have been interrupted by the causeway. Some reports indicate increased pollution of the waters immediately offshore, but at the moment, there seems little to dampen the northwest's appeal.

Getting around

Getting around St Lucia's northern tip is relatively easy, since frequent **buses** run the length of the coast between Castries, Gros Islet and Cap Estate. Marked Route 1a, they leave from the Marketing Board behind the Central Market on Jeremie Street. Schedules are difficult to determine, as the buses tend to leave whenever they are ready, rather than at fixed times, but count on at least one departure every hour from 6.30am until 10pm. You'll pay EC$2 to travel

from Castries to Reduit Beach, Rodney Bay Marina or
Gros Islet. If you're travelling from farther afield, you'll have
to change buses at Castries. If you don't have a car and
would rather avoid public transport, the most hassle-free
mode of transport is to hire a **taxi**. From downtown
Castries to any of the resorts along the northeast coast,
expect to pay around EC$50.

RODNEY BAY AND REDUIT BEACH

Map 4, E7–F7.

Named **RODNEY BAY** after eighteenth-century British
commander George Brydges Rodney (see p.84), the current incarnation of this former American army base is a
compact but fully fledged tourist resort, sandwiched
between the glorious **Reduit Beach** and the shops and
yachting facilities of **Rodney Bay Marina**. The mangrove swamp that once separated the villages of Rodney
Bay and Gros Islet (see p.81) has been replaced by a man-
made harbour channel cutting between the two settlements, which opens out into a deep-water lagoon dotted
with bobbing yachts. From the Castries–Gros Islet
Highway, the main road into town (look for the sign to
Rodney Bay) is on the left side, just south of the harbour
and marina – if you can see the marina on the left, you've
gone too far.

The settlement itself is quite small, and as most of its few
roads lead to the beach, you'll find that it's difficult to get
lost. Most of the activity is split between the beach and the
Rodney Bay Marina. A shopping mall cum yachting haven,
the marina is widely accepted as among the finest in the
Caribbean, with plenty of slips and full services for boaters
as well as restaurants, banks and gift shops. The complex is
also a good spot for booking **watersports**: numerous operators are based here, and activities range from scuba diving,

deep sea fishing and pleasure boat cruises, to windboard, sailboat and motor craft rentals. At the south end of the marina, just after you turn into Rodney Bay from the highway, you can hop on a rather touristy **ferry** to Pigeon Island (see p.87), run by West Coast Ferries (✆452-8079; US$10). As taxis and buses will get you there for a fraction of the cost, the ferry is more a fun ride than a necessity. From their booth next to *The Lime* restaurant in town, the Rodney Bay Ferry (✆452-0087) also offers day-long picnic trips to Pigeon Island for about US$45.

For details of accommodation in Rodney Bay and Gros Islet, see pp.160–164.

Behind the marina lies the original reason for Rodney Bay's growth into a tourism epicentre: the inviting, easily accessible **Reduit Beach**, around 1km long and among the prettiest on the island, with a wide swath of fine white sand, a generally calm surf, a few boats moored out in the bay and views of Pigeon Island to the north and the coastal hills to the south. Usually packed with the oiled bodies of soon-to-be-burnt sun worshippers lined up on their loungers like fallen dominoes, the beach is not exactly secluded, however. Unsurprisingly, it's also lined with places to stay, many of them large-scale but low-lying concrete blocks sitting directly, and intrusively, on the beach, and their proximity adds to the general crowded feel. The beach hotels provide chairs and umbrellas for their guests to use – if you're not staying on the bay, you can rent **beach equipment** from Sonya's at the north end of the beach: chairs and umbrellas are each US$10 per day. There are also several **bars** and **restaurants** dotted along the shore, as well as some of the island's more celebrated entertainment spots and **clubs**, most of which are concentrated in a small area at the south end of the beach (see p.182).

RODNEY BAY AND REDUIT BEACH

Admiral George Rodney

Admiral George Brydges Rodney (1718–1792) looms large in the history of the West Indies, particularly in the bloody history of the French-British conflict over possession of key islands. Rodney entered the British navy in 1732 (at the age of 14) and distinguished himself in his late 20s by leading forces in British naval victories in Martinique – by 1778, he had become an admiral.

By 1782, Rodney had established part of his naval force at the Gros Islet harbour, today's Rodney Bay. From military observation points at Pigeon Island he was able to scrutinize French activity off the coast of northern Martinique. In April of that year the French fleet, under Admiral François de Grasse, sailed from Martinique, intending to join forces with their Spanish allies at Cap François, Haiti, and thereafter sail for Jamaica to attack Fort Charles, one of the largest British strongholds in the West Indies. Rodney countered by sailing his fleet to the Dominica Passage, between Guadeloupe and Dominica, where he cut off and engaged de Grasse's force. A fierce three-day battle ensued, known as the **Battle of the Saints** after the Guadeloupean Iles des Saintes archipelago. The British were victorious; de Grasse and seven French vessels were captured, effectively breaking the back of the French effort in the Caribbean, and winning Rodney the title of baron, bestowed on him by King George III of England.

GROS ISLET

Map 4, E6.

A small fishing village of a dozen streets gathered around an often debris-filled beach, **GROS ISLET** sits just across the harbour channel from Rodney Bay. Bordered by an undistinguished jumble of rickety, rust-roofed wooden homes, the narrow and sometimes crowded streets are lined with vendors selling fresh fruits and vegetables rather than tourist and craft items. Though the town is pretty quiet during the week, tourists and locals pour in each Friday night for the popular **street party** or **jump-up**, as it's locally known. This is the village's main attraction, and everyone pulls out all the stops for some serious revelry. The area around main drag **Dauphine Street**, which runs perpendicular to the Castries-Gros Islet Highway to Bay Street and the sea, is blocked off to make way for the partygoers and the armies of snack vendors peddling everything from barbecue to fried fish, conch kebabs and cold beers. The bars throw open their doors, speakers are set up on street corners and loud music is pumped into the night. The crowd, a mix of St Lucians and tourists, starts to gather about 10pm or so, and the action continues until the early hours, consisting mainly of moving between vendors and dancing as best you can with a beer in one hand and a juicy barbecued chicken leg dribbling down the other. It's a raucous atmosphere, with a sexual undertone to the bacchanalian excesses, but with local police posted here and there to keep an eye on things, the jump-up is generally a good-natured affair. However, a seedier side has developed in recent years. There will inevitably be drunks and hustlers amongst the crowd, and you might be offered highly illegal substances. If you're a woman, you should resign yourself to being approached – it's probably unwise to attend alone. However, if you leave your valuables at the hotel and refuse to buy or accept anything that seems suspect, potential problems should be minimal (for more tips on how to deal with unwanted attention, see p.40).

For more on the Gros Islet street party, see p.201.

Some hotels will bus guests to the party, but it's better to arrange for a taxi driver to pick you up at a specified time, or you'll have to rely on the rather sketchy bus schedule.

Though there is little to distinguish Gros Islet in terms of architectural merit, one building worth a look is the imposing **St Joseph the Worker Roman Catholic church** on Church Street, a block north of Dauphine Street. It's an ornate structure with a cement facade, built in 1926 on the site of a church destroyed by a 1906 earthquake. There's also a **public library** on Marie Theresa Street across from *Daphil's Hotel*.

Dotted with fishing boats, drying nets and small vendor huts as well as some unappealing detritus, the thin public **beach** along **Bay Street** is generally quiet, and passable for swimming – for better beaches, however, make the short trip to Reduit Beach at Rodney Bay town, or the causeway beach at Pigeon Island on the north side of Gros Islet. If you want to **stay** in Gros Islet, there are several guesthouses along Marie Therese and Bay streets, while the local restaurants scattered around town are basic but offer authentic, satisfying Creole fare (see Chapter Nine).

CAS-EN-BAS AND AROUND

Map 1, F1.

Just past Gros Islet, a dirt track known as the Cas-en-Bas Road strikes off the coastal highway toward **CAS-EN-BAS** itself, a small settlement on the remote east coast that's worth visiting for its string of secluded **beaches**, devoid of lifeguards (but safe for swimming) and usually deserted. The Cas-en-Bas turnoff is on the east side of the highway, across from the Gros Islet turn and just north of a Shell petrol station. You can walk to Cas-en-Bas in about an hour, probably a more appealing option than negotiating the endless mucky potholes by car (in the wet season, you'll need a 4WD).

The main road from the highway to Cas-en-Bas ends at the ocean, and it's here that you'll find the first of the beaches. Long and wide with some shady spots under the trees, and an outlying reef taming the rougher waters of the Atlantic, the beach offers marvellous swimming and is likely to be empty or at least uncrowded, although a small beach bar is occasionally open. A more secluded spot lies ten minutes' walk north, along an easily identifiable trail that hugs the rocky, cactus-strewn coastline. Look out for a track that goes back down to the water and you'll find **Secret Beach**, a smaller, very private patch of white sand sheltered by sloping hillocks and volcanic cliffs. A few more minutes' walk north along the coastal path brings you past an open field to another path striking toward the sea and to **Donkey Beach**, an isolated spot of honey sand. It takes around thirty minutes to walk to the beach, and you're unlikely to come across anyone save a few fishermen working their nets.

A half-hour walk **south** of Cas-en-Bas along the rugged and unmarked coastal path brings you to the beach at **Anse Lavoutte**, favoured by **leatherback turtles** as a secluded spot for egg-laying between March and July. If you want to witness this spectacle for yourself, it's best to join one of the organized turtle watches at Grande Anse, a few kilometres further south (see p.132).

PIGEON ISLAND NATIONAL HISTORIC PARK

Map 1, E1. Daily 9am–5pm. EC$10 or EC$30 for a 10-day pass; children under 12 EC$1.

Back on the east coast, the 45-acre **Pigeon Island National Historic Park** is an exposed, hilly spit of land striking into the ocean just north of Gros Islet; confusingly, though, it's not an island at all, having been linked to the mainland via a causeway since the 1970s. Today, it's one of

St Lucia's most popular relaxation spots, a combination of recreation park, concert venue, historic site and tourist trap with the added bonus of several excellent beaches. The island has served as a base for several notable inhabitants, from the Arawaks, who are alleged to have left behind clay pottery, to the infamous pirate François Leclerc, also known as Jambe de Bois or Wooden Leg (see p.91). In 1778, Pigeon Island was fortified by the newly arrived British colonials, and it was from here that Admiral Rodney launched the attack against the French which effectively ended their domination of the Caribbean.

When African slaves were given their freedom by French Republicans following the French Revolution, imminent British repossession of the island combined with fear of re-enslavement spurred them into action. Tagged as the "**Brigands**", the Africans banded together to create a minor rebellion of their own, razing plantations and even taking brief possession of the heavily fortified Pigeon Island before signing a peace treaty in 1798. Since then, the cay has served variously as a camp for indentured East Indian labourers and a quarantine station for patients afflicted with the tropical disease yaws, and had a brief incarnation as a whaling station between 1909 and 1925. In the 1970s, the entire 45 acres were designated a national landmark and afforded the protection of the St Lucia National Trust. The buildings were restored, the causeway was constructed, and Britain's Princess Alexandra opened the park to the public on February 23, 1979, the day St Lucia gained its independence.

Visiting the park

Turning west from the Castries–Gros Islet Highway along the causeway, at the exit signposted for the complex, the first part of the park that you'll pass is a long and wide public **beach**, set opposite the village of Gros Islet and forming the northern fringe of Rodney Bay. At around 1km long, it's one of St Lucia's longer seashores, and one of the calmest – you'll rarely encounter rolling surf. Snorkelling is decent along the main stretch, and if you follow the beach toward the main part of the park, there are several more good, though rocky, spots to don mask and flippers. This long swath of sand is popular with St Lucians on weekends, so expect some crowds, but there is plenty of space for parking, some shaded areas to sit, and vendors selling cold drinks, fruit and barbecued food. However, the construction of a 300-room Hyatt resort in 1999 has drastically altered the aesthetics of this once wide-open seashore, as the resort has effectively sectioned off its own piece of sand and split the beach in two.

Once you've passed the main gate, paid your entrance fee and collected a free map of the island (there's also a large and informative map on a sign board just past the entrance), the **Pigeon Island Museum and Interpretive Centre** is on your right, just past the crumbling ruins of the old officers' kitchen and itself located in the old officers' mess. A mini-museum of the island's chequered past, the one-room centre is worth a brief look, and has displays of Amerindian axes, clay bowls, flint and shell tools and antique colonial furniture; a twenty-minute video presentation describing the history of St Lucia in a nutshell is available. The centre's gift shop sells history pamphlets and books as well as a rather expensive selection of the usual souvenirs and locally produced rum.

Past the Interpretive Centre, the south side of the island is peppered with the remains of the **military barracks** and **encampments** built by the British, including gun batteries, a powder magazine, a lime kiln and what's left of the British Admiral's Fort Rodney. As most of these ruins comprise crumbling brick walls with no roofs, or steps leading to foundations devoid of buildings, you'll need a little imagination to visualize just how well fortified a bastion

Pigeon Island must have been. Some structures are more intact than others, such as the thick-walled powder magazine to the left of the entrance and the old cooperage near the beach on the south side of the island, which now holds toilets. You can explore the ruins via the marked **walking trails** which traverse most of the island, but some of the decaying structures have signs warning visitors off. Every May, impromptu stages are set up in the open spaces among the ruins to host **St Lucia Jazz Festival** concerts; folk performances, local comedy shows featuring Caribbean storytellers, Christmas concerts and monthly music concerts are also held here. Also along the southern shore and reachable via one of the trails is a **military cemetery**, laid out at one of the island's few pieces of flat land. Shaded by tall trees, the weatherbeaten grey and white monuments date back to the late eighteenth century, and commemorate British soldiers and sailors who died in defence of St Lucia.

For more information on the park and Jazz Festival, call the Pigeon Island National Landmark offices (©450-8167 or 450-0063); see also p.198

On the waterfront south of the fortifications, there's a small dock where you can catch the rather expensive tourist ferries (EC$25 one-way) to Rodney Bay Marina. Nearby is Pigeon Island's only eatery, the *Jambe de Bois* restaurant (see p.189), good for sandwiches and cold drinks – save your appetite for some of the better restaurants in the area, however. Two small but appealing **beaches** equipped with toilets and shower facilities lie to the east of the ferry dock. Both are shallow and sheltered by rock jetties which provide calm water, and there are plenty of shady spots under the trees. All of Pigeon Island's beaches are particularly popular on weekends, when cruise ship passengers ferried in from Castries add to the usual crowd of local people enjoying a day out.

François Leclerc

One of Pigeon Island's more colourful past inhabitants was **François Leclerc**, a French sea captain turned freebooter nicknamed Jambe de Bois for his suitably piratical **wooden leg** (there's no record of how his limb was lost). Leclerc arrived in the Caribbean sometime around 1550, and used Pigeon Island as a strategic, protected hideout and base for five years. He is believed to have pulled off some sort of truce with the habitually aggressive Caribs, and is known to have captured at least four cargo ships in his time; survivors of these sea battles were either killed or invited to join his buccaneer crew. He often sank the barren hulks of the ships he stripped for supplies, and legend has it that he secreted **treasure** somewhere along the northern shore of the island, near Pigeon Point. He moved on sometime after 1554, but no records exist of his fate.

Several prominent hillocks dominate the island north of the military buildings; of these, 110-metre **Signal Hill** is the highest. A marked trail leads right to its base, and from there, it should take about fifteen minutes to reach to the peak. It's easy to understand why Signal Hill was designated Pigeon Island's main lookout post: the perspective affords panoramic views south to Gros Islet and the outskirts of Castries, and north over the expanse of the St Lucia Channel to the island of Martinique.

CAP ESTATE

Map 4, F2.

A couple of minutes' drive past Pigeon Island, the coastal road winds a precipitous route to **CAP ESTATE**, a conspicuously upscale residential area distinguished by large villas and estates dotted into the hills east of the highway. The coastal views from anywhere along the road are expansive and compelling: the resort below is the all-inclusive *Odyssey St Lucia*, which dominates the pretty **Bécune Bay**. The main way into the beach is through the resort, which charges EC$175 per person for use of the beach and the all-inclusive hotel facilities for the day (10am–1am). As the rate covers watersports, lunch, dinner, drinks and evening entertainment, it's not a bad deal. The beach is also accessible by an obscure path found off the highway to the south of the hotel, but even though Bécune, like all beaches in St Lucia, is free for all to sit on, you might feel uncomfortable if you're not in possession of one of the wrist bands provided by the hotel to identify their guests. You won't be allowed to use bathrooms, water fountains, beach chairs or umbrellas and will probably be subject to the scrutiny of hotel staff.

For details of accommodation in northern St Lucia, see p.159.

If you're after an ocean swim and some excellent snorkelling, but would rather avoid the hotel, head for **Smuggler's Cove**, a protected, cliff-lined, white sand beach at the north, or back, entrance to *Odyssey St Lucia*. It's accessed from the highway – go past both *Odyssey St Lucia* and the *Le Sport*, and the steps that meander down a steep hill to the beach are on the right. Though Smuggler's Cove is maintained by *Odyssey St Lucia* and boasts a hotel-run beach bar (non-guests will need to bring their own refreshments), there's far less sense of intrusion from the hotel – no entrance fees or wrist bands are required, and you'll share the sand with only a few guests.

Back to the main road, to the south of the Cap Estate homes and across from the *Odyssey St Lucia* is the **St Lucia Golf and Country Club**, the island's only public course and a good one to boot – for more information, see p.213.

CAP ESTATE

SALINE POINT AND THE NORTHERN TIP

Several rough roads that strike off the highway between the *Odyssey St Lucia* and *Le Sport* hotels lead into the hills of St Lucia's northern tip, and to **Saline Point**, home to yet more large homes and vacation villas. Some of the peaks here reach as high as 150m and afford stunning coastal views. Saline Point is not the northernmost promontory of the island, however: that honour goes to remote **Pointe du Cap**, a few minutes further along the coast – there are no signs, but you'll know you're there when the road ends, replaced by the ocean thundering below. From here, St Lucia's nearest neighbour, Martinique, is just 40km away to the north.

Several dusty, unmarked dirt roads head east from Saline Point and Cap Estate toward **Pointe Hardy** on the east coast. Low-lying and scrubby enough to cope with the area's aridity, the liberal quantities of acacia thorn bushes, cacti and prickly pears are markedly different to the lush greenery of vegetation elsewhere on the island; though you're unlikely to encounter one, the area is also home to a non-venomous boa constrictor, locally known as *tete chien*, which is dark with black and yellow patches. Essentially, though, Pointe Hardy's desert-like quality means no tourists, no fences and no admission charges, and the area is ripe for exploration. The St Lucia National Trust are in the process of developing a conservation and eco-recreation site here (call ©452-5005 for an update), and there are several ad hoc **walking trails** lacing the area. Originally created by fishermen and farmers, the trails are not marked but are easy to follow, meandering around small hillocks and along the coast. To walk them, wear sturdy hiking shoes, and you'll need to bring lots of sun repellent and water. If you don't want to go it alone, several companies offer **guided tours** of the area aboard 4WD vehicles (see p.33).

Soufrière and the west coast

T he **west coast** of St Lucia is appealing for its pretty bays, its rural quality, and, in parts, for its decided lack of tourist traffic. You can search out isolated waterfalls, swim in secluded bays and visit peaceful fishing villages, all without the commercial feel of the northwest coast, but towards Soufrière, a host of popular managed attractions lend a more bustling quality to the region.

Less than ten minutes south of Morne Fortune and clustered around one of the Caribbean's most photographed coves, **Marigot Bay** is high on glamour but low on visitors, and the settlement is little more than a handful of hotels and restaurants, most accessible solely by water taxi. South of Marigot is **Roseau valley**, noted for its wide river and extensive fields of bananas; as the home of the nation's largest **rum distillery**, it's also an essential stop if you're interested in the production of the archetypal Caribbean spirit. Gathered around neat village greens and waterfronts lined with brightly coloured fishing boats, **Anse la Raye** and **Canaries** are convenient starting points for excursions to **waterfalls** in the nearby hills, accessed by easy or rigorous hikes.

The largest west coast settlement is the enduringly popular **Soufrière**, a small, unaffected and typically West Indian town that dwells in the shadows of the imposing **Pitons** and offers easy access to the island's celebrated central forest reserves (see Chapter Seven). Just outside the town are the bubbling, odoriferous **Sulphur Springs**, vaunted as the world's only drive-in volcano and the most popular managed attraction that St Lucia has to offer. The land to the southeast of Soufrière was once taken up by massive sugar plantations, and many of the old estates have been opened up as tourist attractions: **Morne Coubaril** gives an interesting insight into the slave era and offers hikes and guided horseback riding excursions into the countryside, while the **Diamond complex** competes with beautiful botanical gardens, waterfalls and eighteenth-century mineral baths.

Getting around

A good, if hilly, road snakes along the southwest coast, making it a relatively easy drive, but **bus** schedules between Castries and Soufrière are a labyrinthine affair. If you're based in Soufrière and want to travel to the capital, infrequent services along the west coast (particularly in the afternoon) mean it's often easiest to first travel south to Vieux Fort, and switch buses there for the final leg of the trip; you should allow the better part of a day for the journey. From Soufrière to Vieux Fort, the bus fare is EC$7, and it's another EC$6 from Vieux Fort to Castries; direct services from Soufrière to Castries along the west coast cost EC$8. Buses also make runs along the west coast from Marigot, Anse la Raye and Canaries to Castries, and you'll pay less than EC$6 to get to the capital. **Taxis** are easy to find, charging EC$160 from Castries to Soufrière, and EC$130 from Soufrière to Vieux Fort.

Marigot Bay to Canaries

Though it's a stretch of only ten kilometres or so, the west coast between Marigot Bay and Canaries is peppered with quiet coastal villages that offer a refreshing alternative to more developed areas of the island. **Marigot Bay** is the only settlement with any kind of tourist infrastructure, and the few hotels and restaurants are perfectly placed to enjoy the natural beauty of this picture-perfect cove. The **Roseau valley** offers the island's only tour of a **rum factory**, as well as some challenging river bank hikes, and at the one-road fishing villages of **Anse la Raye** and **Canaries**, you can buy delicious snacks of tiny *titiri* (fish fried whole) or head into the interior for a freshwater swim at several **waterfalls**.

MARIGOT BAY

Map 1, D6.

The west coast highway scoots through winding, hilly terrain and passes the signposted turnoff for **MARIGOT BAY** some 5km south of the capital; if you're travelling by bus, it's worth asking the driver if he'll make the three-minute detour down to the bay. There's no real town here – a fistful of luxury hotels strung along the north and south sides of the bay make up the main body of the settlement, and Marigot is not the island's busiest spot. The secluded feel is probably the main attraction for many, though, and it's a fine place to head for a relaxed swim and to take advantage of some dazzling panoramic photo opportunities. With massive, lushly vegetated hills enclosing the sea on three sides, Marigot's classic tropical appeal has long been recognized and has not escaped the notice of Hollywood –

the bay was the setting for the 1967 film *Doctor Dolittle*, starring Rex Harrison. The sheltered inner lagoon, **Hurricane Hole**, is one of the best-protected natural yacht harbours on the island, and Marigot's waters are permanently dotted with boats of all shapes and sizes, some owned by the local Moorings charter company and others belonging to the "yachtie" crowd who congregate here.

For details of accommodation in Marigot Bay, see p.165.

From the coastal highway, Marigot's steep access road descends through the hills for about 2km before ending abruptly at the compact waterfront. To the right is the ever-crowded jetty of the **Moorings Marina**, an adjunct of the *Club Mariner Hotel*, and clustered around the complex are the small **police station**, a **customs and immigration** office for incoming yachts, a **taxi stand** (©453-4406) and the *Chateau Mygo* restaurant and shop. Set a few metres back from the waterfront are entrances to the brace of small hotels set high in the hills overlooking the bay (see p.165). Though a sign above the marina jetty reads "Welcome to the *Marigot Beach Club*", the club and its **beach** (the bay's best swimming spot) are actually a few hundred yards across the bay, accessible 24 hours a day via a small ferry boat (EC$2.50 return); the five-minute trip takes you directly to the palm-lined seashore. Slung along a short and thin promontory that juts into the bay from the hotel restaurant, the beach is nonetheless spacious, with calm surf, plenty of shade and good snorkelling to its west side. Refreshments are available from *Doolittle's* restaurant and bar, and the hotel also runs a watersports concession, from which you can rent snorkelling equipment and the like. However, the pseudo-Rasta guys who hang around pestering people to buy illegal substances don't do the place any favours. There's another slender stretch of sand at the *Club Mariner*, but it's far less appealing.

MARIGOT BAY

ROSEAU VALLEY

Map 1, D6.

South of Marigot Bay, the highway winds and dips through the sharp west coast hills to the next settled area, **ROSEAU**, a fertile lowlands valley extensively planted with fields of bananas and dotted with small settlements. The wide **Roseau River** runs right through the centre of the valley, and on its south side (and right on the highway) is the **Roseau Sugar Factory** (*Ø*451-4258; Mon & Wed 9.30am–4pm; US$8), St Lucia's largest rum distillery and the home of fine St Lucian rums Denros, Bounty and Old Fort. Though the factory would originally have used local cane as the raw material for its spirits, much of the sugar used today is imported from Guyana these days, usually in the form of molasses. The excellent half-hourly walking **tours** cover the processing of raw cane to molasses and, finally, rum, and explain modern methods of fermentation and distillation. Some twenty rums and liqueurs produced here are laid out for tasting at the end.

To the east of the factory is a series of **waterfalls** along the Roseau River, but as agricultural chemicals from the banana plantations have been found in the water, swimming is inadvisable. The trip to the cascades makes a pleasant walk in itself, but you'll have to go with a guide – there are no trails as such, and the terrain can get pretty rough. Following the banks of the river is not advisable as there are several spots where you have to detour away from the water, and you'll want to avoid traipsing through private property. To find a reliable **guide**, you can call the forestry department in Castries (*Ø*450-2231) on the off-chance that a ranger will want to take you, or ask around once you're at the valley; several local people will take visitors to the falls for around US$25 per person.

ANSE LA RAYE AND CANARIES

Map 1, C6–B8.

South of Marigot Bay, the highway winds past two typical coastal communities. Both **ANSE LA RAYE** and **CANARIES** are centred around small beaches bobbing with wooden fishing boats. Though there's not much of interest in either settlement, to the east of both are rivers studded with waterfalls which offer a refreshing alternative to saltwater swimming.

About 2km south of Roseau, **Anse Raye** is bisected by the west coast highway, which becomes the village's main drag once you enter town. Crowded with vendors sitting behind haphazard piles of fruit, the narrow streets that spread back from here are lined with somewhat weather-beaten homes, and though the town is pretty and the people generally welcoming, there's not much to stop for in terms of compelling sights. A small and neat town green fronts a small **beach**, chock-full of brightly painted fishing boats and drying nets; you might also see fishermen hauling in the flat, long-tailed skates after which the village is named.

Spanned by a small metal bridge, the **Anse la Raye River** empties into the ocean just south of town, and a fifteen-minute walk along its banks from the bridge brings you to a fifteen-metre **waterfall** with natural swimming pools at the base and a flat area for lounging and picnicking. Way off the conventional tourist track, the falls are mostly used by young kids from the village.

A further 4km south along the highway is the signposted turnoff for the small fishing village of **CANARIES**, thought to have been named after the Arawak *kanawes*, or clay cooking pots, which have been found in the area. Once you've cast your eye over the boat-dotted beach, head south to the six or so **waterfalls** along the **Canaries River**. Though – as with the falls on the Roseau River – forestry department rangers might be persuaded to act as guides (see p.98), the simplest way to find someone to take you there is to ask around the village; you'll pay at least US$25 per person. South of the river is the proposed St Lucia National Trust camping site at **Anse la Liberté** (see p.153), but as there are no roads in, you'll have to walk to the site or take a boat from the Canaries waterfront, which will cost about EC$5.

Soufrière and around

Officially established in 1746, **Soufrière** is the oldest town in St Lucia, and was the island's capital under French rule. Naturally framed by hills and dominated by the looming, conical Pitons – twin volcanic peaks thrusting straight out of the sea to the south of the town – Soufrière's deep **bay** is extremely picturesque, particularly when viewed from the hilly coastal roads as you enter town from the north or south. This unspoiled allure has often drawn the attention of film producers: scenes from *Superman II*, *Water*, and the more recent *White Squall* were shot in and around town.

Soufrière is perfectly placed for **day-trips** to popular **natural attractions** and **plantation tours**, which are all within minutes of downtown and easily accessed via public transport. The Soufrière surrounds also boast some marvellous **beaches**, many of which have black sand left over from past volcanic activity, and the local waters contain some of St Lucia's prettiest **reefs**; in 1994, a marine park was created here to help preserve the delicate ecosystems and to alleviate the pressure put on marine resources by hotels, diving operators and fishermen attempting to feed a growing population. Though Soufrière is generally an unpretentious kind of place, it's heavily visited and is not unaffected by tourism. You'll probably be approached by craft vendors and would-be guides, and some local people will ask for a couple of dollars for giving directions, but the attention is not overpowering and is easily dealt with by a polite "no thanks" if you're not interested.

Taxis and **buses** heading north to Castries and south to Vieux Fort, the east coast and, ultimately, the capital cluster around the town square and the waterfront; the latter is also the place to hop aboard the convenient **water taxis** which traverse the area: boats service all of the nearby bays, many of which are difficult to access from the land without your own car. Water taxis also offer **sightseeing trips** to Castries and back. At US$120 for two, the forty-minute trip is a bit pricey but exotic as hell. One-way, trips (no sightseeing) for four or more people cost US$25 per person.

SOUFRIÈRE TOWN

Map 5.

The largest settlement of the southwest coast, **SOUFRIÈRE** is a quiet place today, charming in its lack of polish and filled with a melange of architectural styles ranging from slapped-together wooden fishing huts to modern cement blocks. Some buildings, particularly those around the town square, recall the ornate facades of French colonial days.

Soufrière's **tourist office** (Mon–Fri 8am–4pm, Sat 8am–noon), on the waterfront and across from the main pier and the Texaco gas station, is a handy source of local information – staff can also direct you to members of the tourism department's helpful **guide corps**. Clad in blue T-shirts that read "Parks and Beaches Commission", they can give walking tours of Soufrière town and help you get oriented.

Soufrière is small enough to explore on foot, and the abundance of jammed one-way streets and the lack of parking render vehicles inadvisable in any case. An obvious starting point is the pretty **waterfront**, a jumble of piers and boat slips where local fishing craft and tourist party boats dock, and where you'll find a small **fish market**, housed in a blue building behind the *Old Courthouse Restaurant*. The **fruit and vegetable market** is a more haphazard affair, with piles of brightly coloured produce sold right on the waterfront and the surrounding streets. Along the north end of the waterfront is a gentrified walkway with ornate streetlights, benches from which to absorb the view and plenty of shade from poinciana trees. The promenade ends at a small **crafts centre** (Mon–Sat 9am–4pm), where you'll probably get the best deals in town on carving, straw hats and the like. Next door is the office of the **Soufrière Foundation**, a regional planning agency working toward sustainable development of the tourism industry; displays inside focus on the local fishing industry and the Soufrière Marine Management Authority, guardians of the Soufrière marine park.

....

**For tours, snorkelling trips and boats to Castries,
contact a member of the water taxi association
at the waterfront.**

....

At the north end of the waterfront, on Bridge Street, the town **cemetery** has been in continuous use since 1743, and the raised cement crypts are faded and occasionally crumbling. North of here, a long, dark sand **beach** is overlooked by a couple of hotels. The beach is pleasant, though not very wide, and you can use the shower and pool of the *Hummingbird* hotel for US$4 – however, there are better places to swim just out of town (see opposite).

....
For details of accommodation in
and around Soufrière, see p.167–170.
....

A block east of the waterfront, and bordered by Bridge Street to the west and Church Street to the east, is the big and grassy **town square**, laid out by Soufrière's original French inhabitants in the eighteenth century, and, notoriously, the scene of numerous **executions** by guillotine during the dark days of the Revolution. It's a peaceful and shady space today, though, bordered by businesses and homes built in the classic French colonial style with second-floor balconies and intricate decorative woodwork. The J.Q. Charles dry goods store at the square's southwest corner is one of the more ornate, with fretwork patterned after snowflakes. Dominating the east end of the square is the **Lady of Assumption Church**, built in 1953 on the site of several older churches destroyed by earthquakes and fire. Soufrière has what might be viewed as bad weather karma: the town was pummelled by hurricanes in 1780, 1817, 1831, 1898 and 1980, and by an earthquake in 1839, while in 1955, half the town was razed to the ground by a huge fire.

Nearby beaches

Map 1, B9–B10.

To the immediate north of Soufrière is the popular **Anse Chastanet beach**, long, wide and presided over by the resort of the same name (see p.167). With a pristine reef within swimming distance, Anse Chastanet offers some of St Lucia's best **snorkelling**. It's also a great starting point for scuba excursions, with several good **dive sites** nearby – there's a dive shop, *Scuba St Lucia*, right on the beach, which rents snorkelling gear as well as scuba equipment. Anse Chastanet is reachable via a hilly dirt road next to the

Hummingbird in about 15 minutes by car or 45 minutes on foot, or by water taxi from Soufrière (US$10 one way). Also reachable by water taxi from town are two pretty and secluded beaches to the north of Anse Chastanet, **Anse Mamin** and **Anse Jambon**.

SOUFRIÈRE ESTATE

Map 5, F5.

With rich, productive soil fertilized in part by past volcanic activity, the Soufrière environs represent some of St Lucia's most heavily cultivated land. The French were the first to set up **plantations** in the area to grow sugar cane, bananas and limes, but today, farming has mostly been reduced to small-scale plots. However, remnants of the plantations still exist: about 2km east of Soufrière town, along the inland road to Fond St Jacques, **Soufrière Estate** is a former eighteenth-century sugar plantation that was originally part of a 2000-acre land grant bestowed by Louis IV to the Devaux family in 1713. The family were responsible for much of the development in the area, and are still prominent hoteliers and landowners.

One of their former estate properties, the **Diamond Botanical Gardens** complex (℗459-7565; Mon–Sat 10am–5pm, Sun 10am–3pm; EC$7), has been refurbished and opened up as a full-scale tourist attraction, and it's well worth a visit, with mineral baths and a waterfall contained in lush grounds. The big, manicured **gardens** are networked by well-marked and easy-to-follow paths and are packed with dozens of labelled tropical species, including brilliant hibiscus in red, pink and white, yellow allamanda, sweet-smelling frangipani trees, the oddly shaped lobster claw and a number of different palms, as well as cocoa trees, tall Norfolk pines and elaborate casuarinas and flamboyants. There's also a small and ethereal Japanese garden, on a side path that loops back to the main walkway, with small and ethereal arrangements of flowers and trees laid out in classic Japanese style. Brochures containing maps are available at the admission desk for an extra charge of EC$2.50.

The main path through the gardens follows the thin Diamond River to a sibilant ten-metre **cascade** fed by a mix of natural streams and underground thermal sulphur springs from the La Soufrière volcano. Splashing over rocks and shimmering with different colours caused by the sulphur content of the water, the falls are nice to look at, but you can't swim here due to agricultural pollution in the water.

Adjacent to the waterfall, the thermal **mineral baths** are built on the site of the original facilities commissioned in 1784 by then-governor Baron de Laborie and Louis XVI for therapeutic use by French troops. The baths were found to contain the same levels of allegedly curative minerals as in Aix-les-Bains in France, and are said to cure ailments such as rheumatism and arthritis. Indeed, some people did – and still do – drink the stuff, believing this to be a more direct route to internal ills. The first spa buildings were destroyed after the Revolution, but you can still see their crumbling remnants in an overgrown hole behind the bath house. Today, you can splash about in the slightly pungent depths of an outdoor pool or in several smaller tubs inside the bath house; the water is cooled from its high in-ground temperatures but it's still comfortably warm. In addition to the main entry fee to the complex, you'll pay EC$6.50 to use the pool and EC$10 for a private bath. Adjacent to the baths is a small bar selling drinks, snacks and sweets alongside souvenirs.

MORNE COUBARIL ESTATE

Map 5, D7. Daily 9am–5pm; EC$15. ℘459-7340.

Less than a kilometre south of Soufrière on the road to Vieux Fort, **Morne Coubaril** is a 250-acre working plantation which has been opened up as a rather questionable tourist attraction. Promising to reveal a "way of life in the good old days", the thirty-minute walking **tours** are conducted by guides clad in eighteenth-century plantation garb – meaning the clothing worn by house slaves. Nonetheless, viewing the fields of cocoa, copra and cassava provides an interesting insight into tropical cultivation, and there's plenty of explanation from the guides.

Also on site are re-creations of thatch-roofed Amerindian huts, as well as a small working sugar mill and several snack and gift shops, but perhaps the best aspect of Coubaril is the guided **hikes**, which include a two-hour trek that starts at the Diamond Botanical Gardens (see p.104), taking in the forest, waterfalls and thermal pools, and ending at the Morne Coubaril hill in the estate grounds. **Horseback tours** of the plantation and the surrounding area are also available. A one-hour ride to a sulphur spring in the hills will cost EC$30, a half-day trip to Malgretoute Beach is EC$50 and a full-day trek including a picnic lunch is EC$70. To arrange rides, call the estate in advance.

LA SOUFRIÈRE SULPHUR SPRINGS

Map 5, E6. Daily 9am–5pm; EC$3.

Misleadingly billed as the world's only drive-in volcano, **La Soufrière Sulphur Springs**, a short drive south of town off the road to Vieux Fort, was a **volcano** some 13km in diameter before it erupted and collapsed into itself around 40,000 years ago. La Soufrière remains active to this day – theoretically, it could erupt any time – but as it is now classified as a **solfatara**, meaning it emits gases and vapours rather than lava and hot ash, a molten shower is extremely unlikely. La Soufrière has long been a place of myth and superstition: despite the fact that there's little evidence of such activity in their culture, old and dubious legends claim that Arawak Indians used the site for human sacrifice, while the querulous but evidently cautious Caribs are thought to have called it *Qualibou*, meaning a place of death.

Turn into the springs at the signed road and you'll know you're in the midst of a volcano – killed off by sulphuric emissions, the vegetation becomes sparse and an eggy odour hangs in the air. After leaving your vehicle in the car park just metres from the most active part of the volcanic area, official (and very informative) guides will walk you up to the viewing platforms that overlook sections of the crater, seven barren acres of steaming, bubbling pools of sulphur-dense water and rocks tinged green and yellow. The pervasive acrid smell is perhaps La Soufrière's most memorable aspect, something like rotting onions in an omelette gone bad. Some years ago, visitors were allowed to walk across the crater, but this practice was stopped when one of the guides fell through a fissure – though sustaining severe burns, he lived to tell the tale. Now, goats occasionally hop across the pools and rocks, cheerfully oblivious of how close they are to becoming stew.

THE PITONS

Map 1, B10, B11.

Towering a kilometre or so above sea level, the anomalous and majestic peaks of the **Pitons** dominate the southwest coast. Visible on a clear day from as far north as the hills of Castries, these breathtaking cones are undoubtedly St Lucia's most photographed feature. Overlooking the south side of Soufrière's harbour, the northern peak is Petit Piton; south of Petit is Gros Piton, wider at the base but similar in height. Maps give various elevations for each of the peaks, some even claiming that Petit is taller than Gros Piton, but the St Lucian government figures of 734m and 798m respectively are generally accepted.

THE PITONS

Beyond their aesthetic appeal, the Pitons offer an opportunity – literally – for high adventure. **Petit Piton** has been scaled in the past, and though the climb is discouraged by local authorities – there are fragile ecosystems to take into account, as well as the inherent difficulty and danger of climbing a near-vertical slab of rock – some still seem willing to clamber up nonetheless. If you do want to attempt this testing two-hour scramble, a guide is essential; you can probably find someone by asking around in the town. You start out along a rocky path which quickly becomes vertiginous; several steep spots require you to use rather tattered (and quite possibly unsafe) ropes. On a clear day, the views from the peak are marvellous: you'll see the neighbouring islands of St Vincent to the south and Martinique to the north, as well as aeroplanes taking off from the island's airports in both Vieux Fort and Castries.

Gros Piton is more manageable for **hiking**, though it's a long and hot ascent nonetheless (bring sunscreen, plenty of water and something to eat), and you'll need to start out in the cool of early morning to ensure that you're able to get back down before nightfall. As the path branches off in several places, a guide is necessary; the Soufrière Regional Development Foundation (☎459-5500) in town will usually be able to find someone for you, and you'll pay about US$40 per person. Depending on your level of fitness, the hike will take three to six hours each way. It starts out low and level along a rudimentary, rocky path and gently ascends until about 300m from the peak, from whereon it's a steep, rocky climb – there are tree trunks and brush to hang on to. The peak itself is a wide, level area with similar views to those atop Petit Piton.

If the so-called "Big Hikes" don't appeal, head for **Anse des Pitons beach**, which separates the twins and provides stunning views of both. Home to the *Jalousie Hilton* resort (see p.192; non-guests are admitted), the beach was recently transformed when the hotel imported US$1 million of gleaming white sand from Guyana to impress its mostly upscale clientele. Several shades lighter than most beaches in the area, the sand looks rather anomalous, and unless the *Hilton* is able to mitigate the forces of nature, it's sure to be swiftly depleted by wave action.

On the south side of the *Jalousie Hilton* property is the **Pitons Warm Mineral Waterfall** (daily 6.30am–7pm; US$1), a pleasantly tepid mix of spring water and thermal volcanic emissions cascading down 30m into a natural pool, which makes for an energizing swim. If you're driving, turn in at the sign for the hotel, from where the route to the falls is marked – you can also take a water taxi to the beach from Soufrière town (US$15).

The south coast

St Lucia's **southern coast** boasts some striking scenery: south of Soufrière, the thin mountain road whirls and dips inland before swinging toward the ocean to reveal a string of typical coastal villages and, ultimately, the island's second largest town, Vieux Fort, all framed by the towering ranges of the central forest reserve. This southwest corner was once an **Amerindian** stronghold, and petroglyphs have been found throughout the area, suggesting a long and fruitful habitation by the Arawaks and Caribs. After Europeans arrived, the area was home to large **plantations** producing bananas, coconuts, cocoa and sugar cane, and some southern villages and towns were minor commerce and shipping centres. These days, the large plantations have been replaced by smaller farms and fishing enterprises.

Despite the fact that nearly all foreign visitors arrive in the south, at Hewanorra International Airport, there's little in the way of tourist activity in this part of the island. Apart from the reclusive *Club Med*, which has laid claim to one of the best beaches, large resorts are almost non-existent. Appealing places to swim are few and far between, and those bays that do line the coast are mostly of the dark volcanic sand that doesn't match up to the conventional stereotype of a Caribbean seashore. In many ways, though, this is the attraction – it's a quieter, more residential part of the island, a world away from the tourism strongholds of the north and west. Indeed, with its beaches, natural attractions and an adequate number of places to stay (all easily accessible from the Hewanorra International Airport at Vieux Fort), it's a mystery why the area hasn't become more popular.

Southwest of Soufrière, as the highway shoots down from the hills to the coast, **Choiseul** is a small and somewhat faded fishing village, wrapped around a picture-postcard shore, and is best known for its Arts and Craft Development Centre, a cooperative where locally made carvings, baskets and pottery are on sale. South of Choiseul, un-hyped tours of the lush 150-acre **Balenbouche Estate** have none of the demeaning costumes and prepared speeches of more contrived, tourist-oriented plantations in busier areas.

As the highway meanders along the southwest coast, the plains and gently sloping hills around **Vieux Fort** stand in stark contrast to the mountainous terrain of the north. While the town itself is crowded and not particularly appealing, the coast east of the city hosts one of the island's finest beaches at **Anse de Sables**, a long, wide stretch of golden sand with mild breezes, popular with windsurfers and sunbathers. Offshore is the fascinating **Maria Islands Nature Reserve**.

Arrival, transport and information

Most visitors arrive in St Lucia at **Hewanorra International Airport** in Vieux Fort, and onward transportation throughout the island is readily available – if somewhat slow – from here.

Your first stop should be the **tourist office** (Mon–Fri 7am–last flight, Sat & Sun 10am–last flight; ℂ454-6644) just outside the arrival area, where you can pick up brochures and maps and get the lowdown on the latest official taxi rates. There are half a dozen **car rental** booths at the airport, open daily from 8am until the last flight, which can arrive as late as 10pm. Also on the concourse, and directly outside the arrival area, is a **taxi** stand – don't bother going downtown to find a taxi, as they cruise the airport and surrounding roads constantly. Taxis to Castries from the airport or anywhere in Vieux Fort travel the wide and slick east coast highway and turn inland toward the capital at Dennery. The **fare** to Castries is EC$125, and the 58km trip takes a bit more than an hour. Vieux Fort to Soufrière is EC$130, and the 42km ride takes forty minutes to an hour, depending upon your driver's tolerance level for steep, winding roads. Vieux Fort to Gros Islet costs EC$150.

Travelling around the south by **bus** is time-consuming and not particularly easy. Like taxis, buses run from Vieux Fort to Castries along the east coast highway, and to Soufrière along the west coast road between 6.30am and 10.30pm during the week; services are much reduced at weekends. **East coast buses** to Castries leave from New Dock Road on the south side of the airport: turn right out of the airport, follow the road past Anse de Sables beach to a traffic roundabout, where you'll see a large soccer field, the Cable and Wireless Building and the bus stand across the road. For **west coast buses** to Soufrière, turn right out of the airport, right at the junction, and the bus stand is on the left at Clarke Street, next to a Shell service station and traffic light. You'll pay under EC$10 to travel to northern St Lucia.

For details of accommodation in the south, see p.170.

CHOISEUL AND AROUND

Map 1, C12.
South of Soufrière, the west coast road meanders through hilly inland terrain, passing several small settlements before

descending abruptly toward the coast and the French administrative Quarter of Choiseul, named for the compact village of **CHOISEUL** itself: the turnoff is on the right, just past a white Anglican church. There's not much to see or do here, save meeting the friendly local people and exploring the pretty waterfront, with its Catholic church and fish market directly on the beach.

Choiseul is bordered to the south by the **River Dorée**, and to the north by a small oceanside settlement called **Caribe Point**, which was home to the last of St Lucia's Caribs until the nineteenth century, by which time inter-marriage had made pure Carib ancestry a rarity. Their descendants still live here today, some in thatched huts reminiscent of traditional Amerindian dwellings. Two minutes' drive north of the Choiseul waterfront is the dark-sand **Choiseul Community Beach**, a wide seashore with plenty of shade under the trees and lots of space for the volleyball court that's a favourite haunt amongst Choiseul's youth. Plans are afoot to build changing rooms and refreshment stands, but at the moment there are no facilities.

South of Choiseul village, the highway runs parallel to a coastal plain for a kilometre or so before entering the small satellite settlement of **La Fargue**, best known for the **Choiseul Arts and Craft Development Centre** (Mon–Fri 8.30am–4pm, Sat 10.30am–2pm; ©459-3226), on the right of the road just past *Miss Lucy's Mini Guesthouse*, and probably the best place on the south coast to buy locally produced crafts. Prices are better than those at the tourist shops of larger towns, and the range here is huge. Artisans display their pottery, mats, carvings, wicker baskets and traditional wood furniture in the main building, while at the back of the complex is a training centre where you might find someone hunched over their pottery wheel, and a workshop that manufactures furniture from mahogany and other local woods. An on-site restaurant sells snacks and drinks.

CHOISEUL AND AROUND |

BALENBOUCHE ESTATE

Map 1, C13. ✆455-1244.

Around 3km south of Choiseul village, the coastal highway crosses the River Dorée and passes the signed driveway which leads into **Balenbouche Estate**, a 150-acre property spread around a charming nineteenth-century **plantation house**, white with a peaked roof and a wraparound porch. Though it's small in comparison to the great houses of other St Lucian estates, the house is large enough to serve as both owner Uta Lawaetz's home and as a **guesthouse** (see p.171). About one third of the grounds are farmed (crops are sold at local markets), and much of the property is permanently shaded by massive calabash, carambola, mango, breadfruit and banyan trees. Also on site are a rusty, non-functional waterwheel dating back to 1780 and the remains of an old plantation sugar mill, now a pile of wood and cut stone shrouded by vines and tropical vegetation.

Balenbouche's grounds stretch right down to the ocean, and a short walk toward the coast takes you to the **Balenbouche River**, which cuts through the estate. Along the shore are several soccer ball-sized rocks with smoothed basins hollowed into their tops, which are believed to have been used by Arawaks as washing stones. The various **petroglyph** sites inland along the river further attest to a strong Amerindian presence in the area. If you want to see them, ask at the great house for a guide; you'll pay about EC$20 per person. From the Balenbouche great house, you can also walk to **Anse Touloulou beach** in about fifteen minutes, following the river banks and ascending a small hillock. The beach is small and secluded with good swimming and gentle surf.

The best way to explore Balenbouche is to join one of the relaxed, informal **walking tours** of the plantation

(EC$10). These are available on request, but call ahead if you want to arrange lunch. If you want to wander around alone or use the beach, a donation of EC$3 is appreciated.

LABORIE

Map 1, D13.

The last village along the road before Vieux Fort, tiny **LABORIE** is skirted by the west coast road and boasts a pleasant bay teeming with fishing boats and a colourful oceanside **market**. On the inland side of the road just north of the village turnoff, a sign points up a steep and rocky hill to the **Le Blanc Nature Heritage** site. Driving up the potholed road to the top of Morne Le Blanc is an act of faith, but the reward for the ten-minute journey is wide views of Vieux Fort and the southeast and west coasts. There are two viewing platforms here and an abandoned building that once served as a craft centre – be careful when climbing the platforms, though, as they appear not to have been attended to for some years.

VIEUX FORT

Map 1, C13.

Jammed with traffic and produce vendors, **VIEUX FORT** is St Lucia's second largest town and its most southerly settlement, a busy commercial centre and the base for businesses which service sprawling **Hewanorra International Airport**, just north of downtown. Both the town and the airport lie on a relatively flat plain that slopes gently toward the north and the south-central mountains, and as the southern tip of St Lucia comes to a point around Vieux Fort, the runway stretches – literally – from the east to the west coast of the island.

Until the early seventeenth century, the area around Vieux Fort was inhabited by the **Arawaks**, who are thought to have grown crops in the fertile plains that spread out beneath the interior mountains. Vieux Fort later came into prominence as a replenishing point for Dutch shippers, who built a small fort east of town on a promontory now called **Pointe Sable** to protect their supplies from the Caribs, thus giving the town its name – "Old Fort" in French. Encroaching European expansion saw the arrival of large-scale cultivation – relatively flat land, an abundance of fresh water and soil rich from volcanic activity made the area suitable for growing **sugar cane**, and by the mid-eighteenth century, there were more than sixty estates in the area. The great plantations lasted throughout the slavery years until the 1920s, when sugar cane prices plummeted in the face of the cheaper and more easily produced beet sugar from other countries. Prosperity came to the area again during World War II, when Allied forces leased 1000 acres of land around Vieux Fort (which encompassed the St Jude Hospital, still in use today), and built a military base and the airstrip which was later enlarged to become Hewanorra. There's still evidence of military construction in the unusually wide roads surrounding the airport, presumably laid to accommodate large military convoys and equipment.

**Reviews of accommodation in
the Vieux Fort area start on p.170.**

Downtown Vieux Fort lies a couple of minutes' drive south of the airport, and the best place to savour the urban bustle is main drag **Clarke Street**, lined with shops and homes embellished with gingerbread fretwork in the classic colonial style. A small, grassy square along Clarke Street has a **bandstand** which serves as an occasional venue for St

VIEUX FORT

Produce market, Castries

Pigeon Island from Cap Estate

Soufrière Sulphur Springs

Walking the Barre de l'Isle Trail

Street scene and murals, Anse La Raye

Reduit Beach

Marigot Bay

Fishing boats, Soufrière

Lucia Jazz Festival performances, while the west side of downtown is bordered by a small, businesslike waterfront where fishing boats pull up on shore, but overall, there's little to do or see.

Each May, St Lucia Jazz Festival concerts are held in and around Vieux Fort – for more details, see p.198.

POINTE SABLE NATIONAL PARK

Map 1, F14, F13 & F12.

Just outside Vieux Fort, the **Pointe Sable National Park** stretches along the southeastern coastline for some 7km, encompassing the **Cape Moule à Chique** promontory, **Anse de Sables beach**, the **Man Kòtè Mangrove** and the **Savannes Bay Nature Reserve**, as well as the offshore **Maria Islands**. Sponsored by the St Lucia National Trust, the park is undeveloped at present – the areas are not yet fully regulated nor particularly well cared for – but the Trust's efforts to preserve the seagrass beds, mangrove swamps and coral reefs are slowly coming to fruition.

Cape Moule à Chique

Map 1, F14.

At the southern outskirts of downtown Vieux Fort, the large and hilly promontory of **Cape Moule à Chique** (233m) juts into the sea, forming St Lucia's most southerly point and framing the industrial port on Vieux Fort Bay, an inlet with storage warehouses and massive docks for large cargo ships. To get to Cape Moule à Chique, drive to the traffic roundabout and bear left onto a winding, bumpy track into the hills, and turn left again at a Cable and

Wireless station. There is a spot to park at the point's working **lighthouse**, where you'll have views of the east coast, the expansive Anse de Sables beach and the two off-shore Maria Islands (see opposite) as well as the interior mountains.

Anse de Sables

Map 1, F14.

Stretching some 2km north from the cliffs of Cape Moule à Chique to Pointe Sable, the **Anse de Sables beach** is the best (and the only) place to swim near Vieux Fort. A favoured spot for windsurfers, the expansive seashore is usually breezy with a mild surf and virtually no trees for shade; there are also no changing and toilet facilities except those at several oceanside bars and restaurants. At the south end of the beach, in the shadow of the looming Cape Moule à Chique, is the **Maria Islands Interpretive Centre** (Mon–Fri 9am–5pm, ✆454-5014), a small natural history centre which is the focal point for the National Trust's efforts on the south coast, as well as the place to arrange a trip to the Maria Islands, which lie a kilometre or so off-shore (see opposite). The one-room **museum** provides an interesting insight into local ecosystems and history, with displays on Amerindian culture (including skeletal remains and a skull found in the area), as well as on mangroves and marine life; the fishing industry section has an example of a traditional dugout canoe called a *gonmyé*. There is no admission charge, but a donation of EC$3 is recommended.

North of the Pointe Sable promontory is the gated entrance to the *Club Med* hotel, which sits on a stretch of sand that's not accessible to non-guests. South of Pointe Sable, at Beanfield, the seashore is known as **Cloudnest Beach**, and there are a couple of hotels and beach bars as well as a small **fish market**. The beach at this end is okay, but as fishermen tend to be busy here, a day at the beach is better spent a few hundred metres south at the section called **Sandy Beach**. Though this is the most popular spot on the beach (particularly on weekends, when townspeople descend), the paucity of tourists along the south coast means that the sand is rarely crowded, and you're likely to share it only with the occasional vendor wandering along selling straw hats or aloe for sunburn. Not content with the sizeable portion of sand that it calls its own, *Club Med* also maintains a sports facility here, from which equipment and beach chairs are doled out to guests only. However, everyone can get a cold drink or use the restrooms at the *Sandy Beach Club* next door, and the nearby *Reef* beach bar rents beach chairs (EC$5 for the day) and windboards (EC$40 per hour) as well as serving decent food.

Maria Islands Nature Reserve

Map 1, F14.

A kilometre or so off the Anse de Sables shore are the two scrubby, windswept cays which comprise the **Maria Islands Nature Reserve**. Both the hilly, 24-acre **Maria Major** and its smaller sister islet, 4-acre **Maria Minor**, are breeding areas for numerous **sea birds**, including the booby and frigate, and are home to two reptiles found nowhere else in the world. About a metre long with dark green and brown markings, the harmless **kouwés snake** (also spelled "couresse") once thrived on the mainland but was eradicated by the mongooses introduced by sugarcane planters to kill off cane rats, mice and snakes; today, *kouwés* live only on Maria Major and number a mere one hundred or so. At around 35cm long with a bright blue tail and a yellow belly, the male *zandoli tè*, or **ground lizard**, is colourful enough to recognize easily; brown with darker vertical stripes, females are less ostentatious.

There's a short but comely **beach** of golden sand on Maria Major, with a **reef** a few metres offshore, making this a good spot for swimming and snorkelling. Several unmarked and unchallenging **trails** loop around the islands, taking you past sparse, cactus-strewn vegetation and rocky shoreline. It's difficult to get lost on such tiny pieces of land, but in any event, no one is allowed on the Marias without an **authorized guide** from the St Lucia National Trust (see below). They will lead you through the trails in search of *kouwés* and *zandoli tè* and will identify the flora and fauna at hand. You're unlikely to see birds nesting, as the islands are closed to human visitors during the May to September season.

Visiting the islands

If you want to **visit** the Marias, you'll need to phone or call in at the **Maria Islands Interpretive Centre** (Mon–Fri 9am–5pm; ℭ454-5014) at the south end of Anse de Sables beach (see p.118). This is the only place to arrange a day-trip conducted by official National Trust guides. Costing EC$80 for one person, EC$58 per person for two or three people, and EC$46 per person for groups of four or more, the trips begin at the centre and consist of walking tours of the islands as well as stops for swimming and snorkelling (bring your own gear). With advance notice, and for an extra EC$25, the centre can also arrange picnic lunches, or you can bring your own.

Though you can arrange Saturday or Sunday trips, the centre is open only on weekdays, and its hours are erratic and subject to frequent change. Though they have no official sanction to do so and are not professional guides (most will simply transport you there and back), local fishermen sometimes take visitors to the islands for about EC$45 per person, but this is not encouraged due to the delicate ecology of the islands; it also undermines the hard work that the

National Trust are doing in the area. Booking an official trip is a far better option – to ensure that the centre is open when you want to visit, call ahead before you set out. Lastly, note that visiting the islands is **prohibited** between May and September, when several species of birds are nesting.

Man Kòtè Mangrove and Savannes Bay Nature Reserve

Map 1, F12–13, G12.

Some 3km from Vieux Fort and just north of Pointe Sable, the coastal highway toward Dennery passes a signposted turnoff marked "Mankote". The muddy dirt track leads 2km toward the shoreline and to the **Man Kòtè Mangrove**, a primary breeding ground for marine life. The swamp comprises red, white and black mangrove trees, which serve as a protected feeding ground for bird and marine life such as egrets, herons, conch and juvenile fish, as well as buffering the land from sea swells. The ecologically sensitive swamps are dense, and the only bit of Man Kòtè that you can visit is a thin **beach** hugged by palms and sea grape trees. Though it's littered with beer cans, picnic remains and ashes from cooking fires (and not a very pleasant spot to swim), the beach is nicely secluded and is slated for upgrading by the National Trust.

A few minutes further along the coastal highway is the roadside Savannes Bay and the **Savannes Bay Nature Reserve**, marked by a small sign. The reserve is basically a large mangrove swamp surrounding a pretty bay which is enclosed by **Saltibus Point** to the north and **Burgot Point** to the south; the small **Scorpion Island** sits at the north end of the cove. Amerindians are believed to have settled in the area, and archeological digs have been undertaken at the north and south of the bay. Sheltered by an outlying **reef**, Savannes Bay forms a protected **breeding**

area for spiny lobsters, conch and numerous species of fish, and it's a prime fishing spot. Though there are no walking trails or organized activities in the area, fishermen selling their catch at the small market on the highway might be persuaded to take you on a trip around the bay to see the swamp from a different perspective.

The east

Churned up by the Caribbean trade winds, the pounding waters of the Atlantic have carved out a rough and jagged **east coast**. Characterized by a lively surf smashing against rocky and cliff-lined shores, the area provides a visual contrast to the more quiescent west. Less suited to farming and fishing, the region is also sparsely inhabited in comparison to the north and west of the island.

There are only two sizeable settlements in eastern St Lucia: 10km northeast of Vieux Fort, **Micoud** is an appealing village wrapped round a diminutive harbour, while slap in the middle of the eastern coastline, the fishing and farming stronghold of **Dennery** is the last port of call before the coastal highway strikes inland toward Castries. North of Dennery, the landscape is distinguished by undramatic, low-lying hills to the west and a decided lack of roads. Tarmac dwindles into rough dirt tracks, and you'll need a 4WD to explore. If you can manage to make it in, though, you'll be rewarded with an excellent plantation tour at **Marquis Estate**, as well as the area's finest **beach** at **Grande Anse**, a sweeping stretch of sand where **leatherback turtles** come to lay eggs.

In effect, the lack of roads north of Dennery prevents unplanned exploration, and the **southeast** is by far the most accessible part of the region. North of Micoud, the coastal highway swings past small villages such as **Mon Repose**; from here, a quick trip into the lush interior brings you to the small but engaging **Mamiku Gardens**. Back on the coast and just north of Mon Repose, sheltered **Praslin Bay** boasts one of the southeast's few safe swimming beaches, and each weekend, the sand is crowded with mostly St Lucian beach devotees. At the northern end of the bay are the two offshore islands which form the **Fregate Islands Nature Reserve**, a sensitive nesting area for the magnificent frigate bird, which can be visited only with St Lucia National Trust guides. Beyond the Fregates, informal tours of **Errard Plantation**'s cocoa groves are worth a trip into the interior.

....

For details of accommodation in the east, see p.172.

....

Getting around

St Lucia's **coastal highway** parallels the eastern shoreline from Vieux Fort to Dennery, where it cuts inland, heading northwest across the island to Castries. The fastest way to travel the 58km between Vieux Fort and the capital, it's also the preferred route for buses and taxis between the two towns. Along the way, east-coast **bus** stops include Micoud, Desruisseaux (in the hills south of Micoud), Mon Repose, Praslin and Dennery, but exploring the coastline by bus is not particularly efficient, as schedules are inconsistent from one day to the next. To travel to the west coast, you'll often need to catch a bus to Vieux Fort for connections to Soufrière and north to Castries – this is a time-consuming route, however. From Castries, buses to the south coast leave from Manoel Street, and coming from Vieux Fort, New Dock Road is the place to catch a bus to Dennery. You'll pay no more than EC$8 for any single journey.

Taxis shuttle up and down the main highway constantly, but in the southeast are easiest picked up in Vieux Fort, Micoud or the Dennery area. Fares from Vieux Fort are roughly EC$125 to Castries, EC$70 to Micoud, and EC$80 to Dennery.

The coast north of Dennery is generally inaccessible in anything other than a 4WD, which can be rented, albeit for a premium. An alternative is to take a trip with one of several tour companies offering excursions in the area (see p.33).

The southeast coast

Though it's a only short drive from the international airport where most visitors first touch down, St Lucia's **southeast** corner is often bypassed, seen only fleetingly from the window of a bus on its way to the more conventionally tourist-friendly resorts of the northwest coast. This is a shame, as there's lots to do and see, and a constant stream of buses and taxis travelling between Vieux Fort and the capital means that it's also easy to get around.

MICOUD

Map 1, G10.

Named in honour of the French Governor de Micoud, who ruled St Lucia from 1768 to 1771, the relatively sizeable town of **MICOUD** spreads back from the sheltered **bay** of **Port Micoud**. The suitability of the harbour to fishing, and the ready availability of fresh water from the **Troumassé River**, which borders the town to the south, are the principal factors cited by archeologists as evidence of intense **Amerindian** presence in the area. Some nine settlements are believed to have existed in the Micoud Quarter, and to have been rapidly abandoned after the arrival of European settlers in the eighteenth century.

Before the coastal highway was completed in recent years, the old east-coast road passed straight through Micoud, typical of St Lucian fishing villages in its numerous compact streets lined with a mix of old homes embellished with West Indian fretwork and modern concrete block architecture. Today, the highway passes about a kilometre north of the village, and a sign marks the turnoff.

Aside from the pretty bay, dotted with fishing boats and churches, Micoud is best known as the birthplace of the island's first prime minister, **John Compton**, though there's nothing to commemorate the connection. The town is also renowned as a particularly enthusiastic focal point for two islandwide religious **festivals** which also take place throughout the island, **La Rose** in August and **La Marguerite** in October. Rooted in the island's syncretic commingling of African and European religious traditions, the festivals celebrate the Roman Catholic saints Rose of Lima and Marguerite Mary Alacoque through religious services, feasts and flower shows as well as costume parades, parties and public performances of traditional songs and dances. Visitors are welcome to observe, or even join in the fun.

MAMIKU GARDENS

Map 1, G9. Daily 9am–5pm; EC$15.

A few minutes' drive north of Micoud, **Mamiku Gardens** (©455-3729) are thought to have been named after the wife of one-time French Governor de Micoud, who owned an estate here in the late eighteenth century;

"Mamiku" is probably a Creolized contraction of her title, Madame de Micoud. By 1796, the property had fallen into the hands of the British, who used it as a military post and command centre for engaging the **Brigands**, escaped slaves who roamed the countryside waging war for freedom. In one of the larger skirmishes, the British engaged the Brigands on the estate property; according to the diary of post commander General Sir John Moore, fifteen British soldiers died and twenty were wounded, and the estate home was burned to the ground. Shamed by the decisive defeat and loss of British lives, Moore later committed suicide. The estate was eventually abandoned and its buildings left in ruins until the turn of the twentieth century, when it was turned into a commercial banana and tropical flower plantation.

Today, the twelve-acre gardens are teeming with brightly coloured exotic blooms such as hibiscus, ginger and heliconia; tree species include the carambola and gommier; the area's distinctive dugout fishing boats are fashioned from the latter. You can explore the gardens via a simple network of short **walking trails**, each with resting spots at suitably beautiful points. One five-minute trail leads to the top of a hill which holds the foundations of the old plantation house and provides extraordinary views of nearby Praslin Bay (see p.128). If you don't stop to admire the scenery, the longest trail will take about twenty minutes to walk. There are no guides for the trails, but you can pick up a free brochure at the entrance, which has a map. Though the paths themselves are short, there's a lot to see, and you'll probably spend a couple of hours exploring. There's a snack bar and gift shop on site.

Mamiku is located on the west side of the highway, between the roadside village of Mon Repose and Praslin Bay. A sign marks the turnoff, from where it's a two-minute drive (or a 5min walk).

MAMIKU GARDENS

Horseback rides through the hills are available from *Fox Grove Inn* hotel at Mon Repose (©455-3271); see p.173.

PRASLIN BAY

Map 1, G9.

A 2km cove split in two by a rocky outcrop, the sheltered **Praslin Bay** offers one of the southeast's few opportunities for a safe ocean swim. Blessed with a gentle surf and plenty of shade, the **beach** at Praslin is long and wide, protected by the narrow bay entrance and enclosed by high hills. As this is one of the nicest swimming spots in the area, it's likely to be busy on holidays and weekends, popular with lively but laid-back young St Lucians. There's no official place to park, so if you're driving, you'll have to find a space at the side of the highway before following one of several paths leading down a precipitous embankment to the beach. There are no facilities, but a few vendors peddle cold drinks and snacks at the weekends. Toward the middle of the bay is tiny **Praslin Island**, which you can visit with an authorized guide from the St Lucia National Trust (see p.33).

Praslin is also noted for its distinctive **fishing boats**, carved out from whole gommier tree trunks and distinguished by their upturned, pointed bows: there are usually a few moored up at the small pier in the centre of the bay.

Fregate Islands Nature Reserve

Map 1, G8. Daily Aug–April 9am–5pm; tours only, EC$48.

Occupying the northern section of Praslin Bay, the **Fregate Islands Nature Reserve** is centred around the two tiny **cays** just metres offshore which are named after the seagoing **frigate bird** that nests here between May and July.

Glossy jet black birds with forked tail feathers, male frigates have distinctive red or bright orange throat pouches which are expanded during mating time to attract females. Also known as the magnificent frigate or the man-o'-war bird, the frigate's two-metre wingspan allows it to remain in soaring and swooping flight for great lengths of time, and it's thought that they even sleep while floating on air currents. However, frigates lack the oily plumage film that allows other seabirds to shed water and resurface after diving, and rather than risk drowning after a plunge into the ocean, frigates feed by skimming the water's surface for fish, or simply by stealing from other birds.

The reserve is also home to several other **bird species**, including herons, yellow-eyed, brown-feathered tremblers and St Lucia orioles, black with orange patches on the belly and underside of the wings. Also occasionally seen on the island is one of St Lucia's larger **snakes**, a dark tan boa constrictor that's locally known as *tête chien* and often attains a length of 4m. Tan with orange, diamond-shaped markings, the poisonous *fer de lance* snake is also found in isolated sections of the east coast, but you're extremely unlikely to see these shy creatures.

As you're not allowed onto the islands themselves, the reserve is best explored on the mainland section via an easy, 1.5km **walking trail** that loops through a changing scenery of thick vegetation to dry spots of low-lying bushes and cacti, passing a **waterfall** that flows in the rainy season, a mangrove swamp and an observation point overlooking the Fregate Islands before returning to base.

The reserve is marked by a sign in front of a small car park on the ocean side of the highway; however, when you get there, you'll probably find the entrance gated and locked. The Fregates are maintained by the **St Lucia National Trust** (©452-5005 or 453-1495), and no one is allowed in without one of their authorized guides, who will conduct **tours** for two or more people; these are included in the entrance fee. If you do find the gates unlocked (and it's best to call ahead if you want to visit), you can look around the **interpretive centre**, a wooden hut in the car park, which has maps and illustrations of wildlife found in the preserve. Despite the inconveniences, the tour is well worth the time it takes to set it up. At extra cost, the National Trust can also arrange transportation from Castries, lunch and a boat tour to the unoccupied **Praslin Island** in the centre of Praslin Bay.

ERRARD PLANTATION

Map 1, G7. Tues & Thurs 10am–3pm; US$40.
Some 3km north of Praslin Bay, on the southern outskirts of Dennery, **Errard Plantation** (©453-4554) is a commercial estate that cultivates mainly cocoa; groves of trees sprout the yellowish oval pods that contain cocoa beans. On request (and for groups of four or more only), estate manager Eugene Dixon conducts four-hour **tours** of Errard's operations, which include an introduction to cocoa processing and a stop at a beautiful 22-metre **waterfall** on an estuary of the Dennery River, a great swimming spot and the highlight of the tour. You'll also get lunch featuring supremely fresh juices made from fruits grown on site.

If you don't fancy the tour or you show up unannounced, you'll be allowed into the property free of charge to have a look around; even so, you should probably call ahead to make sure someone is there. Alternatively, Spice Travel (©452-0865) in Castries organize twice-weekly tours for US$65 per person, which includes return transport from anywhere on the island. To get to Errard from the east coast highway, look for the sign on the north side of the Dennery Bridge. Turn off and follow the road overhung with electric wires – this leads directly to the property.

Dennery to Marquis Estate

The main drawback of the **northeast** coast is its lack of driveable **roads**. A few kilometres north of the relatively sizeable settlement of **Dennery**, they peter out completely, and inconveniently. The most practical way to access the area is from the northwest coast via the Allan Bousquet Highway, which runs inland from Choc Bay (see pp.68–69) and connects to several laborious dirt tracks which meander toward the coast. These demand a 4WD, but if you can get your hands on one (or you opt instead to leave the driving to a tour company), you'll find several extremely comely bays, including **Grande Anse**, where a planned government park and reserve will soon afford protection to the giant **leatherback turtles** which come here to nest. The St Lucia Naturalist Society organize eco-sensitive **turtle watches** at the beach throughout the March to July breeding season. North of Grande Anse, on Marquis Bay, is **Marquis Estate**, a large plantation that's open for pre-arranged **tours**.

DENNERY

Map 1, G7.

Once known as Anse Canot, and later as Le Grand Mouyaba, **DENNERY** was given its current name by the French, following a 1768 visit to the town by then-Windward Islands governor, Count D'Ennery. The village extends back from a deep and protected **bay**, with uninhabited **Dennery Island** at its northern tip. A major export centre for agricultural produce throughout the nineteenth century, Dennery is a fishing and farming community today, and – since the addition of the large, Japanese-funded Daito Complex and Pier processing facility – it's also one of St Lucia's busiest **fishing** centres.

The **town** itself is a jumble of compact streets with a few bars but nothing much in the way of tourist sights. The looming white and rust coloured **St Peter's Roman Catholic Church** sits a block from the seafront. Built from stone and mortar between 1789 and 1841, the church is one of the oldest on the island.

GRANDE ANSE

Map 1, G4.

Around 10km north of Dennery, the wide, windswept **Grande Anse beach** boasts more than two kilometres of blonde sand set against a backdrop of cliffs and hills covered with dry vegetation. Once part of a plantation estate, the bay sits in the middle of an area slated to become a new **national park** comprising several other nearby beaches, such as **Petite Anse** to the north and **Anse Louvet** to the south. Amerindian **petroglyphs** and artefacts have been found within the proposed park area at Petite Anse, Grande Anse, Tortue Point and Anse Pouvert, and the area is rich with historical significance.

The **beach** itself is inviting and often empty of visitors, but as strong winds usually churn up a rough surf, swimming can be risky. The main attraction of Grand Anse, though, is the annual visit of sea **turtles**. The bay is the primary St Lucian nesting spot for endangered **leatherback** turtles, which also lay their eggs at Fond D'Or, the next bay north of Dennery. Though hawksbill and green turtles (also protected in St Lucian waters) also nest at Grande Anse and at other beaches around the island, the leatherbacks prefer to make an annual journey to Grande Anse's apparently inviting sands to burrow out egg-laying chambers, and they

The leatherback turtle

The rarest – and the largest – of the sea turtles that frequent Caribbean waters is the **leatherback** (*Dermochelys coriacea*), which has a shell as long as 1.5m and a body weight of up to 680kg; a male weighing in at 1144kg is the biggest specimen on record.

Named for their triangular **carapace** or shell, which is covered by a layer of leathery brown and black skin rather than the hard scales of other species, leatherback turtles have changed little in their 65 million years of existence. However, they face **extinction** today. Leatherbacks are still hunted by humans, and ocean pollution and accidental entrapment in fishing nets kill thousands. Their laying beaches are being transformed into tourist resorts or diminished by sand mining, and as their main food is **jellyfish**, they often mistake floating plastic waste for food – the immense male mentioned above was found with 24 plastic bags in his intestines.

Nesting females are among the most implacable mothers on earth, leaving the ocean every two to six years only to lay eggs. Under the cover of night, they lumber up the sand and burrow the hole into which they lay 80–85 eggs before returning to the sea for about ten days. Females will go through this process up to a dozen times during a laying period, depositing as many as 800 eggs during the March to July season. These incubate for as long as three months and produce fully functional **hatchlings**, which emerge at night and paw their way to the surf. Only an average 1 in 1000 baby leatherbacks survives the six years it takes them to reach maturity.

come in their hundreds – in 1997, a record figure of 116 females were counted. During the leatherback egg-laying season, roughly March to July, St Lucia Naturalist Society volunteers head out to Grande Anse to monitor nesting

THE LEATHERBACK TURTLE

females and protect the turtles and their eggs from predators and from human poachers. Periodic upgrades of the roads to Grande Anse have led to an increase in the latter, while the excavation of large quantities of sand for use in building work has threatened both the turtles' habitat and the beauty of the beach. For now, though, leatherbacks are still coming to Grande Anse, and you can witness them nesting for yourself by joining one of the **turtle watches** organized by the Naturalist Society (see below).

Despite the regrading, most of the roads to Grande Anse remain dirt and gravel tracks that become impassable after rains. A sedan car might make it, but a 4WD is a safer bet, and it's a good idea to ask locals about current conditions. Access is most often easiest from the west coast at Choc Bay (see pp.68–69), via the paved Allan Bousquet Highway. At Babonneau, turn off onto the gravel and dirt track that leads to the village of Desbarra, from where a single track leads down to Grande Anse. The eleven-kilometre ride from Choc Bay can take up to ninety minutes.

Turtle watch

In conjunction with the Department of Fisheries, the St Lucia Naturalist Society organize an annual programme of **turtle watches**, allowing around 1000 visitors each season to experience the stirring spectacle of leatherback turtles laying their eggs. Since the mid-1980s, the watches have been conducted by turtle authority Jim Sparks of the Naturalist Society. Currently, the watches take place on Saturday nights only; at about 4pm, groups of around thirty people assemble at Derek Walcott Square in Castries, are taken out to Grande Anse and return by 8.30 the next morning. Once at the beach, you settle in to a rustic tent village and take turns at patrolling the beach. Whenever a turtle is spotted, you'll be called to have a look.

The turtle watch trip costs EC$15, which covers transport and tent expenses only; you'll have to bring your own food and drinks as well as a flashlight, toilet paper, and warm clothing, as nights can be cool and breezy. The watches are becoming very popular, and to ensure a place, it's best to contact Jim Sparks well in advance (PO Box 2170, Gros Islet, St Lucia, WI; ℂ452-9829 or 452-8900).

MARQUIS ESTATE

Map 1, G4. Tues, Wed & Thurs; US$56.

Just north of Grande Anse, the sprawling **Marquis Estate** is bordered by the **Marquis River**, with **Marquis Bay** at its eastern edge. First established in 1760 as a sugar plantation, Marquis is no longer a working farm, but remnants of past activities form the basis of its latest incarnation as a tourist attraction. The estate has served as the home of several former governors, and was **fortified** to protect its illustrious occupants – at the peak of a hill near the estate house, several rusting cannons overlook the Atlantic. Also on site are ruins of a chapel and other plantation buildings.

The current owners of Marquis Estate are the Atkinson family, who conduct walking **tours** of the property, pointing out local flora and fauna and recounting the history of the estate and surrounding area. Tours include a look around the old sugar works as well as a trip to the banana fields for an explanation of the fruit's growth cycle, and a cookery demonstration in which local foods are prepared for your lunch. There's also a quiet guided **boat ride** down the Marquis River to the sea. Rough surf at Marquis Bay means that swimming is not recommended, but beachcombing can yield some interesting shells and other assorted flotsam.

Tours must be **pre-arranged**, either by contacting the estate directly (ℂ450-5436), or through Sunlink Travel in Castries (ℂ452-8232). If you simply show up, you'll be

The interior forest reserves

Stretching across the island's central and north-central interior, the vast, uninhabited and irregularly shaped **St Lucia Forest Reserve** comprises the 19,000 acres of rainforest and dry forest which are maintained by the government's forestry department. The entire reserve is divided into smaller, loosely demarcated **sub-regions**, most still referred to by the names given in the early colonial days when forest trails were the shortest route between St Lucia's east and west coasts. These days, though, most people who venture in do so for pleasure rather than necessity. Arrestingly beautiful and teeming with exotic flora and wildlife, the forests offer an absorbing alternative to the sun-and-beach culture of coastal resorts.

Essentially, the interior reserves have been created to protect the island's last portions of unfarmed virgin forest and the often rare animals and birds that inhabit them, but the area is also used for recreation, and many of the reserve's **hiking trails** have been opened up to the public. Of these, the easiest is probably the **Union Nature Trail** near Babonneau in the northwest. Though it isn't actually in the

Common forest flora and fauna

The **topography** of the forest reserve is immensely varied, ranging from relatively flat plateaux to steep summits. The peaks and valleys of the central mountains are covered by rich, green woodlands, and the high mountain altitudes create rain and nourishing mist, generating prolific semi-rainforest woodlands and primordial "montane" **rainforests** of moss-covered branches groaning with epiphytic bromeliads, orchids and even mushrooms.

Among the trees are numerous species of **birds**, of which the most famous is the **St Lucia parrot** or *jacquot*, immediately recognizable by the brilliant blue feathers on its head, colourfully matched by green wings, a yellow tail and a red spot at its breast. In the past, the *jacquot* was often hunted for its feathers, and numbers had reached a low of 150 by the late 1970s. Conservation programmes were initiated in 1978, and today, there are thought to be more than 350 living in the forest reserve.

Though the numbers have been reduced by hunting, the most common **mammals** in the forests include the shy **agouti**, a dark brown or black rodent resembling a large rat with muscular hind legs, and the cat-sized **manicou**, an opossum with a long snout and a rat-like tail. Other animals include rats, mice and the **mongoose**, a ferret-like creature that feeds on smaller rodents, snakes and domestic fowl.

Reptiles include the endemic St Lucia **tree lizard** and the **pygmy gecko**, tiny and light green; dark brown and black with a row of spiny protrusions along the neck, the prehistoric-looking **iguana** grows to as long as 2m and is found in trees where it feeds on leaves and fruits.

reserve proper, it's a pleasant stroll, and the small, on-site **zoo** provides a thorough, if rather depressing, overview of local wildlife. Another unchallenging walk, both in terms of access and difficulty, is the **Barre de L'Isle trail**, which begins at the side of the Castries-Dennery highway and leads for 2km or so along the north-south ridge that bisects this section of the island. The **Edmund Reserve** in the west-central section contains the island's highest peak, 950-metre **Morne Gimie** (also called Mount Gimie) as well as several worthwhile hiking trails of various lengths and levels of difficulty: the **Enbas Saut trail** is a fifteen-minute walk to a swimmable waterfall, while the **Edmund trail** itself is a more laborious cross-island trek. The east-central **Quilesse Forest Reserve** is accessible at the **Des Cartiers Rainforest** section, just inland of Micoud on the east coast, and its short and relatively easy main trail provides a succinct introduction to tropical rainforests.

The most popular of the interior hikes are the Barre de L'Isle, Edmund Reserve and Des Cartiers Rainforest trails, but even these are unlikely to be teeming with tourists – hiking is not high up on many people's Caribbean itineraries, and you'll most likely have St Lucia's hiking trails entirely to yourself.

Hiking practicalities

A division of the awkwardly named Ministry of Agriculture, Lands, Forestry, Fisheries and Environment, the **Forestry and Lands Department** (℡450-2231) maintains St Lucia's protected forest reserves and all of the hiking trails within them. The division also determines public access (some parts of the interior are restricted) and provides trained **hiking guides**. A flat fee of EC$25 covers access to a single trail as well as the services of a guide, vital for exploring ecologically sensitive and challenging hikes such as Morne Gimie or the Edmund Reserve cross-island walk. At extra cost, the forestry department can also

HIKING PRACTICALITIES

arrange **transport** to the trails, but travel arrangements might depend upon a minimum number of people on the walk; tours are often subcontracted to commercial companies, which means you'll be traipsing along a quiet rainforest trail with twenty other people and are unlikely to get the most out of the experience. As the forestry department is understaffed (ranger stations at the start of the trails are sometimes un-manned) and, at times, poorly organized, you should always call a few days in advance to arrange guides or transport, and it's also well worth clarifying the details of forestry department transport before you book.

If you do want to hike, remember that though you're in the mountains, it will be hot, so you should bring sunscreen and a hat as well as plenty of drinking water and some snacks. Light clothing is fine and sturdy footwear is a must for all hikes.

Getting to the trails

Unless you elect to arrange your transport with the forestry department or take a tour with Castries-based commercial companies such as Jungle Tours (℗450-0434) or Sunlink Jeep Safaris (℗452-9678), travelling independently to the interior forests is not an easy proposition. Public transport is limited, but you can reach some trails by taking an inland **bus**, which will cost EC$5 or less. Services run directly to the start of Union and Barre de L'Isle walks, but for most of the hikes listed in this chapter, you'll have to take a bus to the nearest town and walk to the start of the trail, often a few kilometres away. If you decide to opt for a **taxi**, make arrangements to be collected at an appointed hour, as you're unlikely to find drivers cruising for fares in the mountains. If you can afford it, renting a **car** is probably the easiest option, and regular sedan vehicles will get you to the start of all the trails listed in this chapter.

UNION NATURE TRAIL

Map 1, E4. Daily 8am–4.30pm, EC$5.

The forestry department's field headquarters is the starting point for the short, easy **Union Nature trail**, and the complex, about half an hour's drive from Castries, also contains a herb garden, a small **zoo** and an interpretive centre, though the latter was under renovation at the time of writing and is not expected to re-open for some time. Usually ensconced in the main office building, rangers are on site every day between 11.30am and 3pm to give **tours** of the centre and the walking trails, but you're free to amble about by yourself during opening hours.

The centre's tiny, neat **zoo** houses some fifty animals common to St Lucia and the Caribbean, but it's a sad affair, with animals pacing, jabbering and generally looking somewhat distressed. Inmates include **vervet monkeys**, light grey in colour with a dark facial "mask", several **boa constrictors**, a couple of **agoutis** and birds such as **macaws**, orange-winged **parrots** and the island's national bird, the **St Lucia parrot** or *jacquot*; as these are rarely seen in the wild, this might be your best opportunity to view a *jacquot* up close, albeit a rather confused and dishevelled specimen.

The **Union trail** begins just to the left of the rangers' office and loops through dry forest that was once planted as a tree nursery, returning back after about an hour of walking if you don't make too many stops. At only 1.6km, it's an easy stroll, with gentle slopes rising to 100m and occasional hillocks to scramble, but it's simple to follow and you don't need a guide. Free **pamphlets** that explain some of the flora along the trail (and in the medicinal garden) are available from the rangers, and common trees such as almond, glory cedar, gommier and calabash are labelled with plaques.

UNION NATURE TRAIL

However, you might want some expert input when walking the shorter path just behind the office, which winds through a small **medicinal garden** where rangers grow herbs used in traditional cures. The *wallwort* leaf, for example, is boiled with milk and imbibed for colds and fever, and the *kasialata* leaf can be rubbed on the skin to stop itching.

To get to the centre, head north along the Castries-Gros Islet Highway for about ten minutes before turning inland toward Babonneau along the signposted Allan Bousquet Highway. There are no signs to signify that you've reached Union, but after a winding 2.5km, you'll see a large fence to the right, which protects the station's agricultural propagation field; turn right at its end to reach the centre. **Buses** travelling the Allan Bousquet Highway leave from Jeremie Street in Castries and will drop you off at the turnoff for the station, but getting back can be more of a problem; services are infrequent, and you'll probably end up walking back to the Castries-Gros Islet Highway.

BARRE DE L'ISLE TRAIL

Map 1, E7. Weekdays 9am–3pm; EC$25.

Literally translated as "island ridge", the **Barre de L'Isle trail** meanders along the north–south ridge which bisects the Central Forest Reserve. It's a worthwhile half-day adventure and provides a good insight into St Lucia's richly diverse topography and mountain flora and fauna: throughout, the trail alternates between a thick overhead cover of trees and wide-open areas with expansive vistas of the mountain ranges south, east and west.

The signposted start of the Barre de L'Isle trail strikes into the forest directly from the central Castries–Dennery highway, a twenty- to thirty-minute drive or bus journey from downtown Castries. Buses leave from Manoel Street in

Castries – tell the driver where you're heading, as he'll know where to drop you. Once you've cleared Morne Fortune and the Cul de Sac Valley, rainforest vegetation becomes evident: the roadside is swathed with bamboo, elephant ferns and dark, towering trees. Opposite the sign marking the start of the trail is a gravel road leading up a hillock to the **rangers' hut**, where you pay your entrance fee and can hire a guide. The hut is usually staffed, but an escort isn't strictly necessary for this easy-to-follow walk; however, a guide will be able to identify bird species as well as trees and plants along the trail, and you might have a better time if you take someone along.

Extending about 2km into the forest (you retrace your steps on the way back), the trail is a hilly but generally easy two-hour hike that alternates between cool, thick forests where the canopies of towering trees block out most of the sunlight, and wide-open hilltops that provide remarkable views of the coast and of Central Reserve mountain ranges, including Morne Gimie to the south. The 438-metre Mount La Combe lies near to the start of the trail, and you can extend your hike by electing to climb it. As you'd expect, the mountain trail is steep in places, but it's only mildly challenging, and the reward for your effort is panoramic views that stretch south, east and west.

EDMUND FOREST RESERVE

Map 1, D10. Daily 8am–4pm, EC$25 per trail.

Spreading over the southwestern interior, the **Edmund Forest Reserve** is a convenient starting point for exploring the rainforests if you're based in Soufrière. The available walks range from an untaxing fifteen-minute jaunt to a waterfall along the Enbas Saut trail, to the more challenging ascent of Morne Gimie, St Lucia's highest peak, or the Edmund trail, a ten-kilometre hike which crosses over the centre of the island to the east coast, passing through the Quilesse Forest Reserve and ending at the Des Cartiers Rainforest near the east-coast town of Micoud (see p.125). Though the Edmund trail was named after a French farmer who owned tracts of surrounding land in the early twentieth century, the many trails through the reserve (some are off-limits to hikers) have existed since the mid-eighteenth century when Soufrière town was first established, and were the primary route between the island's west and east coasts.

The 8km drive to the Edmund Reserve will take about an hour from the west coast. You should be able to make it in a regular rental car, but if it's rained recently, a 4WD may be necessary on the last stretch. From Soufrière town square, take the inland road to Fond St Jacques, bypassing the turnoff to Morne Coubaril Estate and the south. The road winds through the small village of Zenon, after which it's another half an hour or so along a considerably more rocky track to **Fond St Jacques**, a tiny rural community (don't expect to be able to stock up on snacks and drinks) and the last village before the formerly tarred road becomes a rocky track leading only to the rainforest. Buses from Soufrière go only as far as here, and if you've travelled in on public transport, you'll have to walk the rest of the way to the rainforest.

The road to the trails turns left off the main road by a zinc-roofed cement bus stop in the centre of the village. After a few minutes, the lush forest flora becomes noticeable: looming, bromeliad-bedecked trees filter the sunlight, while elephant ferns interspersed with broad-leafed dasheen plants planted by farmers smother the side of the road. To the north, the peak of Morne Gimie is occasionally visible through breaks in the trees, and there is a noticeable increase in humidity.

After a twenty- to thirty-minute drive, depending on the condition of the road, a wooden forestry department **ranger station** is the first indication that you're in the reserve itself; it's usually staffed by forestry guides and officers who'll collect your entrance fee.

Enbas Saut trail

To the immediate left of the rangers' hut is a sign marking the start of the **Enbas Saut Waterfall trail**, an easy, self-guided, fifteen-minute walk down a sloping track which brings you directly to the cascade. The water is clean and you can swim in the deep pool, and usually there's not another soul in sight. Flanking the trail and the waterfall are a profusion of ferns, as well as towering mahoe, gommier and mahogany trees which may, if you're lucky, provide a roost for the rare and colourful St Lucia parrot.

Edmund trail and Morne Gimie

The more formidable ten-kilometre **Edmund Trail** begins from the main access road to the rainforest, about ten minutes' walk beyond the ranger station. It's a fairly demanding four-hour walk – more if you linger and stop for bird-watching – and a forestry department **guide** is highly recommended; side trails branch off the main route and it is easy to get lost. You may be able to hire a guide at the ranger station, but to be sure, it's best to call the forestry department in Castries a few days before you plan to hike (℡450-2231). Starting **early** is also advisable: you'll benefit from the cool of the morning, and it's a good idea to allow plenty of time for stops. If you elect to walk the whole trail, you'll need to arrange for someone to drop you at the start and collect you at the trail end; otherwise, you can simply turn back when you're ready. If you do walk the length of the trail, relying on public transport is not really a viable option: you'll spend more time on buses (or waiting for them) than on the trail itself.

The trail is mostly over flat terrain, with some small streams and crevices spanned by foot bridges, and despite the length, this is a relatively easy-going hike with stunning scenery and lots of **birdwatching** opportunities – keep your eyes open for the *jacquot*, as well as orioles, white-breasted thrashers and various hummingbirds. For much of the time, you're in the shadow of Morne Gimie, St Lucia's highest peak at 950m, and in places, the panoramas of the mountains are vast.

Several **alternative routes** branch off from the main Edmund trail, some leading toward the south and others to **Morne Gimie**. If you want to tackle the latter, you'll need a specialist guide, which can be arranged through the ranger station. However, it's an arduous and time-consuming hike that isn't often attempted.

DES CARTIERS RAINFOREST

Map 1, E9–10. Daily 8am–4pm, EC$25.

The **Des Cartiers Rainforest** in the southeastern interior is handy for those staying in the southern half of the island, and its easy **trail** provides a good introduction to St Lucia's interior riches as well as saving you the hassle of trekking in to less accessible parts of the reserve. The four-kilometre trail follows old military roads laid by the French during World War II; it's well marked, and a guide isn't necessary. From the reserve, you can also link up with the Edmund Reserve trail, which threads through the centre of the island toward the west coast (see p.145); however, it's a rigorous four-hour trek, and a guide is essential.

The rainforest lies some 10km into the mountains from the east-coast highway, and the Des Cartiers trail begins at a small, sporadically staffed forestry department **interpretive centre** where you pay your entrance fee and can peruse the displays on rainforest plant species; adjacent are toilets and a roofed picnic hut. Though the Des Cartiers trail is more than 300m above sea level throughout, it's actually a relatively flat, looping hike that skirts the **Canelles River** and brings you back to the ranger station in about two hours. There are several marked lookout spots, said to be haunts of the *jacquot*, and sweeping views can be had of the south and east coasts from a couple of higher elevation points. At the northern stage of the loop, there's a marked turnoff for the Edmund Forest Reserve trail.

The primary route into the Des Cartiers reserve is a signposted turnoff a minute or so north of the east-coast village of Micoud (see p.125). The road is in good condition, passing through the tiny settlement of Anbre and running parallel to a small branch of the Canelles River. Local people swim in the water, but as it's polluted, taking a dip is not really advisable. From the coast, it's a thirty-minute drive to the boundary of the reserve. **Buses** into the eastern interior are extremely infrequent, and if you don't have a rental car, you're best off hiring a **taxi** if you want to walk the Des Cartiers trail; you'll pay about EC$60 one-way from Vieux Fort, and you should arrange for the driver to wait or come back and collect you.

DES CARTIERS RAINFOREST

Accommodation

ince the early 1980s, St Lucia has aggressively beefed up its tourism facilities, and now boasts around 3900 guest rooms island-wide. Accommodation runs the full range, from luxury **all-inclusives** and medium-sized **family hotels** to terrific, inexpensive **bed and breakfasts** and **guesthouses**. Though the majority of establishments are moderately sized and priced, large resorts with a hundred rooms or more are now becoming the bedrock of the industry, which has caused some local contention.

Most of the island's accommodation is located along the **west coast**, where the calm waters lend themselves to conventional resort activities. North of Castries, the stretch of coast from **Vigie Beach** to **Cap Estate**, including the heavily visited areas of **Rodney Bay** and **Gros Islet**, is known as the "Golden Mile" – here you'll find some of St Lucia's best beaches and the greatest concentration of accommodation. South of Castries, another crop of hotels springs up at the secluded and quiet **Marigot Bay**, less than 8km from the capital. There's little tourist buzz here, just a tranquil bay dotted with moored yachts and a handful of small hotels and restaurants. In the southwest, the historic town of **Soufrière** now hosts several exclusive resorts as well as smaller, more economical hotels and guesthouses. Further south at **Vieux Fort**, the relatively few hotels tend to be functional rather than flamboyant, servicing nearby Hewanorra International Airport. With fewer beaches and an infrastructure still based on fishing and farming, the **southeast coast** offers limited but worthwhile accommodation choices, convenient for excursions into the interior forest reserves. Note that all accommodation reviewed in this chapter is marked on the maps at the back of the book.

When **booking** accommodation, it's important to bear in mind that St Lucian hotels generally levy a ten percent **service charge** and an eight percent **government tax**, which are either included in quoted rates or tacked on to the final bill at the end of your stay. All-inclusive hotels include all taxes and service charges in their rates, as do most small guesthouses (though some disregard them entirely). Medium-sized hotels can go either way. As the price codes used in this guide are based on the quoted rate – which may or may not include taxes – it's essential to check when booking whether you'll be subject to additional charges or not.

It's worth knowing that **toll-free** hotel booking numbers generally connect you to an outside reservation service rather than the hotel itself. You may get a more favourable rate, as well as more accurate and up-to-date information about airport transfers, amenities, special packages and promotional rates by calling individual properties direct.

Lastly, if you need to see pictures before making a booking, **tourist offices** on the island and abroad (see pp.21–22) will send out brochures and comprehensive lists of approved accommodation, as will the **St Lucia Hotel and Tourism Association**, PO Box 545, Castries, St Lucia, WI (©452-5978, fax 452-7967), and the **Inns of St Lucia**, 20 Bridge St, Castries, St Lucia, WI (©452-4599, fax 452-5428), a marketing group representing nearly three dozen small properties offering simple, comfortable and moderately priced accommodation.

ACCOMMODATION

Accommodation price codes

All accommodation listed in this guide has been **price-graded** according to the rate charged for the cheapest double or twin room during **high season** (mid-December to mid-April). In the low season rates can be reduced by up to forty percent, and it's not unusual to get smaller discounts in the quieter spring and autumn months at either end of the high season.

① less than US$30	⑤ US$150–189
② US$30–69	⑥ US$190–229
③ US$70–109	⑦ US$230 and above
④ US$110–149	

All-inclusives

A concept pioneered by the *SuperClubs* and *Sandals* chains of Jamaica (*Sandals* has two resorts on St Lucia), **all-inclusives** are precisely what the name implies: resorts where your room, all meals, snacks, drinks, sports, amenities and tips are included in the price. You'll usually only have to pay for things like laundry and certain sports such as scuba diving.

The advantage of all-inclusives is the clarity of exchange. You needn't be bothered by tipping, arguing over who pays for dinner or secreting loose change in your sandals on the beach. The disadvantage is one of local economics and attitude. As everything is already paid for, there's little incentive to leave the resort, which of course antagonizes the local restaurateurs, bar owners and watersports operators, who rely on tourism to make a living. For the most part, the local community (except for employees and suppliers) sees few monetary benefits from their all-inclusive resort neighbours. Recently, though, a few all-inclusives, such as *Odyssey St Lucia*, have begun to address the problem by offering vouchers for local restaurants and bars, a good arrangement for both the local restaurateur and for the guest – if you're staying two weeks at a resort, do you really want to eat there every day?

Still, all-inclusive resorts enjoy a booming business, and their offers can be tempting, particularly when combined with airfare and ground transport. However, it's important to read the small print before booking to check which activities are included; and remember that the rate quoted will often be for one person based on double occupancy. For more details on packages, see Basics.

Renting a villa

Essentially multi-bedroom houses for rent, **villas** are scattered throughout the island and are often the most convenient and inexpensive option for families, larger groups and those who want to get away from the tourist stream. Rates often include maid and cooking services, rental cars and other amenities; split several ways, a villa can work out to be extremely cost-effective. Count on spending US$1000–3000 per week in high season.

For **rentals**, contact Tropical Villas (PO Box 189, Castries, St Lucia, WI ℰ452-8240, fax 452-8089); Island Link Villa Service (PO Box 370, Castries, St Lucia, WI ℰ453-6341, fax 453-6303); or Villa Apartments, on The Morne in Castries, which lists moderately priced apartments for long- and short-term stays (PO Box 691, Castries, St Lucia, WI ℰ452-2691, fax 452-5416).

Camping

Camping has yet to catch on in the Caribbean, and at present, it is not a fully sanctioned activity in St Lucia. There's only one proposed campground (and even this may not be open yet), at **Anse la Liberté**, south of Anse la Raye. Maintained by the National Trust (©452-5005, fax 453-2791), the site is remote and inaccessible by car – you have to hike in carrying everything you'll need. It's near to a small, somewhat rocky beach, and is perfect if you want to get away from it all. Future plans include permanent tents on wooden platforms, barbecue grills and communal showers and toilets, but be sure to call ahead and check what's available before you set out.

The government allows some camping in selected areas of the interior **forest reserves** (covered in Chapter seven). There is no system as such, but permission is granted on a case-by-case basis by the Forestry and Lands Division, Environmental Education Unit, Ministry of Agriculture, Castries (©450-2231). It's free to camp at present, but the Forestry Division has indicated that payment will be required in the future. Again, you have to hike in (and out) carrying all your provisions and equipment. If you strike out without permission, you'll make the Forestry Division unhappy to the point of possible prosecution; additionally, certain sections of the forest are not suitable for camping; if you are hurt or in trouble out there, no one will know where you are.

It's also highly inadvisable to pitch a tent on the beach, unless you're with an organized group such as the Grande Anse turtle watch (see p.134). As well as being potentially dangerous – you are exposed to theft and other crime –you might well be camping on private land without permission.

CASTRIES AND AROUND

Unless you have a yearning for busy streets and traffic, there's no compelling reason to stay in **downtown Castries**, and you'll find that most of the hotels are more pleasantly located on the harbour or bays immediately north and south of town; these also have the advantage of easy access to city transport.

ACCOMMODATION

The **hills** surrounding the capital hold several small properties, distinguished by their reasonable rates and well-regarded restaurants. You won't be on a beach, but you'll have the benefit of refreshing breezes, not to mention views of the harbour, town and neighbouring islands. North of downtown, **Vigie Peninsula** has several excellent restaurants as well as accommodation used mostly by businesspeople. Along the Castries–Gros Islet Highway north of Castries, a wide range of resorts, from all-inclusives to smaller hotels and guesthouses, sit on or close by the beaches of **Choc Bay**. Just north of here, the sheltered Labrellotte Bay and Bois d'Orange hills host several of the island's finest hotels. Public transport to all spots in and around Castries is plentiful and inexpensive.

Auberge Seraphine

Map 3, C6. Vieille Ville Bay, Pointe Seraphine ℂ453-2073 or 453-2075, fax 452-7001.
Set on a small inlet on the west side of Pointe Seraphine and favoured by business travellers for its easy access to downtown Castries. The spacious, upscale rooms are appropriately businesslike, too, with porch, a/c, cable TV and hair dryer. Upstairs, above the restaurant, is a patio with a pool and sun deck. An unexpected attraction is the tree in front of the parking lot, which provides a roost for hundreds of cattle egrets in the early evening. ③.

Beach Walk Inn

Map 3, F4. Choc Bay ℂ451-7888 or 452-2523, fax 453-7812.
Opposite Choc Bay beach on the east side of the busy and noisy Castries–Gros Islet Highway, this small guesthouse is right in the thick of it for restaurants, beach bars and shopping. Some rooms come with refrigerators, some with kitchenettes, and there are one-, two- and three-bedroom apartments for larger groups. ②.

Bon Appétit

Map 3, B8. Morne Road, Morne Fortune ℂ452-2757.
The best aspect of this four-room guesthouse in the hills is its small but highly regarded French/West Indian restaurant (see p.179). The rooms are basic, clean and secure, each with private bath, TV and fan; rates include breakfast. ②.

Caribbees Hotel

Map 3, D6. La Pansee ℂ452-4767, fax 453-1999.
High on a hill on the east side of Castries, and within easy distance of the capital, the multi-storey *Caribbees* has sixty ample, reasonably priced rooms and a pool. There are complimentary shuttles to local beaches, and stunning views of the town from the restaurant as the lights twinkle on in the evening. ②.

Dubois Inn

Map 3, B8. Morne Road, The Morne ℂ & fax 452-2201.
Mrs Dubois's four clean, simple rooms (one with three beds) have a fan and access to shared hot water. There's a convivial common room/patio with cable TV, and appealing views of the harbour and Vigie Peninsula from the grounds and several rooms. Next door is the family's small but exceptional West Indian restaurant, which is lavishly adorned with award-winning decorations each Christmas.
No credit cards. ②.

East Winds Inn

Map 1, E2. Labrellotte Bay ℂ452-8212, fax 452-9941.
An elegant all-inclusive set on a private beach (great snorkelling and watersports), this is a true escape; during the rainy season, the horrific condition of the road in from the highway increases the sense of retreat. The luxury bungalows have refrigerators and TV with VCR, and there's a pool, bar, shops and an excellent restaurant. ⑦.

Green Parrot

Map 3, B8. The Morne ✆452-3399 or 452-3167, fax 453-2272.
Slightly tatty and infused with the air of a former hot spot, this
55-room inn in the hills south of Castries offers escape from
the beach scene and a chance to wallow in the coolish breezes
drifting up the hills. The restaurant's West Indian cuisine is a
real draw, as is its alfresco seating with views of Castries below.
There's a pool, and the hotel provides complimentary transport
to local beaches. ③.

Orange Grove Hotel

Map 1, E2. Bois d'Orange ✆452-9040 or 452-0021, fax 452-8094.
Sixty-two spacious, comfortable rooms in a renovated French
colonial plantation set atop a breezy hill, halfway between
Choc Bay and Gros Islet, an area well known amongst bird-
watchers for the variety of species. There's a pool (overlooked
by rooms 201–204), several restaurants and a complimentary
four-times-daily shuttle to Choc Bay. ②.

Rendezvous Hotel

Map 3, D5. Malabar Beach, Vigie ✆452-4211, fax 452-7419;
in US ✆1-800/544-2883.
Sprawling seven-acre all-inclusive on Malabar Beach, with
tons of watersports and amenities, including hot tubs, two
pools, tennis, fitness rooms, scuba diving, golf and nightly
entertainment as well as a couple of restaurants and bars.
The vast rooms are luxurious and seem tailor-made for what
the name implies; only mixed-sex couples (and no children)
are accepted. ⑦.

Sandals Halcyon and Sandals St Lucia

Halcyon: **Map 3, F4.** Choc Bay ✆453-0222, fax 451-8453;
in US ✆1-800/726-3247.
St Lucia: **Map 3, A7.** La Toc Bay ✆452-3081, fax 452-1012;
in US ✆1-800/726-3247.

The beaches at these two *Sandals* resorts are wide with calm water, and the all-inclusive *Sandals* formula for success – generic island fun – is no different here than in Jamaica, where the chain originated and gained its reputation for excellent food, extensive sports facilities and luxury rooms. *Sandals St Lucia* is the larger of these two, and guests can access the beaches, restaurants and amenities of both via an hourly shuttle. Note, however, that *Sandals* allows only mixed-sex couples; no kids and no singles. ⑦.

Seaview Apartel

Map 3, D5. John Compton Highway ✆452-4359, fax 452-6690.
Overlooking the George F.L. Charles Airport and within two minutes' walk of Pointe Seraphine, the location is congested and noisy but convenient for public transport. Both the furnished apartments and the standard double rooms have private bath, a/c, TV and phone, and there's a restaurant on site. ②.

Sundale Guesthouse

Map 3, F4. Sunny Acres, ✆452-4120.
Paul Kingshott's small, tightly run guesthouse on a side road near the Gablewoods Mall is scrupulously clean, inexpensive and within walking distance of Choc Bay's beaches. Rooms have verandahs, fans and private bath with hot water, and the three one-bedroom apartments can sleep four at a push. There's a communal lounge with TV and VCR, and breakfast is included in the rates. No credit cards. ②.

Windjammer Landing

Map 1, E2. Labrellotte Bay ✆452-0913, fax 452-0907; in US ✆1-800/743-9609.
Sprawled over 55 hillside acres on and above Labrellotte Bay, with accommodation ranging from luxury rooms to white-

stucco, self-contained villas, some containing up to four bedrooms, some with private pools, all with stunning views. Golf carts shuttle you around between the site's four restaurants (one is beachside), four pools and the beach, which offers watersports. The kid-friendly atmosphere is unusual and refreshing. Rooms ④, cottages ⑦.

Wyndham Morgan Bay Resort

Map 3, G2. Choc Bay Ⓒ450-2511, fax 450-1050; in US Ⓒ1-800/996-3426.

Despite the 22 acres, 238 rooms, armies of guests and the corporate name, the all-inclusive *Wyndham* manages to be warm, welcoming and a great choice for families. Staff are efficient, rooms are large, the grounds are impeccable and the two restaurants are faultless. Watersports are on offer at the adequate beach, and land activities include tennis, volleyball, croquet and aerobics in the large fitness centre; golf and scuba diving cost extra. ⑥.

GROS ISLET AND THE NORTH

As St Lucia's main tourist heartland, the island's northern tip is plentifully supplied with large resorts, medium-sized hotels and inexpensive guesthouses, the majority located in the "Golden Mile" between **Rodney Bay** and **Gros Islet**. Despite the area's popularity, accommodation is no more expensive than in less busy parts of the country, and proximity to beaches, watersports, golf, shopping, restaurants and tour companies make it the ideal spot if you like to be in the thick of it all. Being so near the capital, public transport is abundant, the coastal roads are good, and there's plenty of opportunity for exploring both the coast and interior (though for the latter, you'll need a rugged, preferably 4WD, car).

Bay Gardens Hotel

Map 4, F9. Castries–Gros Islet Highway ℄452-8060, fax 452-8059.
Set in almost incandescent lemon-lime buildings gathered around a free-form pool and lushly landscaped gardens, the a/c rooms have verandahs, TV, coffee-makers and a minibar. Those on the second floor overlooking the pool have the best views. Reduit Beach is just down the road, accessible by a free shuttle. ③.

Candyo Inn

Map 4, E8. ℄452-0712 or 452-4599, fax 452-0774.
Close to some of the island's best swimming spots and restaurants (it's 5min on foot to Reduit Beach) yet surprisingly quiet; you won't be bothered by crowds. Decorated with florals, pinks and potted plants, standard rooms and apartment suites are sizeable; the latter come with kitchenettes and separate sitting rooms. There's a small pool and snack bar. ③.

Gib Motel

Map 1, F2. ℄452-9528, fax 452-0963.
Five clean, tidy, inexpensive rooms a couple of minutes inland of Rodney Bay (look for the sign). Some have gas stoves and fridges, others multiple beds (room 3 can sleep five); all have cold-water showers, and there's a pool on site. ②.

Harmony Marina Suites

Map 4, E8. ℄452-8756 or 452-0336, fax 452-8677;
in US ℄1-800/742-4276.
One of the original hotels on Rodney Bay, right on the marina, and around 200 yards from Reduit Beach. The 30 luxurious and comfortable suites have fridges, coffee-makers,

hair dryers, etc. Twelve rooms have kitchens, but the marina-side restaurant, the *Mortar & Pestle*, is one of Rodney Bay's best (see p.186). ③, ④ with kitchen.

Islander Hotel

Map 4, E9. ☎452-8757, fax 452-0958; in US ☎1-800/223-9815.
Straightforward and functional with a pool, restaurants, bar and free shuttles to nearby Reduit Beach. The plain rooms and apartments with kitchenette are rather uninspiring, but all have small fridges and a/c. Two kids under twelve can stay free in the same room as two adults. ③.

Palm Tree Hotel

Map 4, F9. ☎452-8200, fax 452-8894.
On the south side of the marina, just off the Castries–Gros Islet Highway, the new, family-run *Palm Tree* is small and comfortable, if a bit sterile. The twenty standard rooms have a/c and TV, and rooms 101 and 104 have views of the pool. There's a restaurant, bar and hot tub as well as a beauty salon offering massage amongst other treatments. ③.

Rainbow Hotel

Map 4, E6. Reduit Beach ☎452-0148, fax 452-0158.
Large and gaudy with rainbow colours splashed all over its lobby and roof, the *Rainbow* has 76 spacious rooms. Most overlook the pool, and there's a restaurant, bar and fitness centre on site. Across the street is Reduit Beach, which puts the hotel right at the centre of things. ②.

Rex Papillion

Map 4, D8. Reduit Beach ☎452-0984, fax 452-9332; in US ☎1-800/223-9868.
The beachside butterfly-shaped pool reveals the owners' determination to drive home their theme, and this is another good spot for relaxing at a pool or beach. The 140 rooms range

from standard (with fan) to deluxe (a/c and views of Reduit Beach). Standard ⑥, deluxe ⑦.

Rex St Lucian

Map 4, E7. Reduit Beach ℂ452-8351, fax 452-8331; in US ℂ1-800/255-5859.

The larger of the two sister resorts on Reduit Beach, offering sizeable rooms with all amenities, restaurants, cafés, tennis and watersports. The big attractions are the beach in front and the plethora of Rodney Bay restaurants. ③.

Royal St Lucian

Map 4, E7. Reduit Beach ℂ452-9999, fax 452-9639; in US ℂ1-800/255-5859.

Right next to its sister property on the popular Reduit Beach, the *St Lucian* has 96 lavish suites and three fine restaurants; the pool, with bridges, a waterfall and interconnecting waterways, is an attraction in itself. A spa was newly installed in 1998 and is one of the best ones on the island. ⑦.

Tuxedo Villas

Map 4, E7. Reduit Beach ℂ452-8553, fax 452-8577.

These ten villas across the street from Reduit Beach have kitchens, a/c and TVs. Two-bedroom, two-bathroom units represent good value for larger groups, and there are one-bedroom villas as well. There's a restaurant and pool on site. ④.

GROS ISLET AND AROUND

Alexander's Guesthouse

Map 4, E5. Marie Therese Street ℂ450-8610, fax 452-5428.

Ten inexpensive, spartan rooms near to the sometimes dirty Gros Islet beach. Two rooms have kitchenettes (others have use of the owner's kitchen to make breakfast), most rooms share the hot-water bathrooms and there's a communal TV lounge. The proximity of the Friday night street party inevitably means some weekend commotion. ②.

Bay Guesthouse

Map 4, E5. Bay Street ✆ & fax 450-8956.

Right on Gros Islet's public beach, convenient for public transport and about a minute's walk from the Friday night street party, this small guesthouse has both adequate standard rooms and studios with kitchens; all feature private bathroom, fans and mosquito nets. No credit cards. ②.

Daphil's Hotel

Map 4, E6. Marie Therese Street ✆450-9318.

Pink, tall and cheap, this ten-room inn is close to the beach, just across the street from Gros Islet's public library. Smallish rooms have private baths, fans or a/c (those on the second floor have ocean or street views) and breakfast is available for US$5. ②.

Glencastle Resort

Map 4, G6. ✆450-0833, fax 450-0837.

Just off the main highway, on a hill above Gros Islet with views of Rodney Bay and its marina, this small hotel has seventeen modern rooms set in a two-storey building around the central pool and deck. It's a bit lifeless, but good value and convenient for excursions to west-coast beaches and the Gros Islet street party. ③.

Golden Arrow Inn

Map 1, F2. Marisule, Gros Islet ✆450-1832, fax 450-2459.

Set on the beach side of the Castries–Gros Islet Highway, but not on the water, these fifteen rooms are rudimentary, with en-suite baths and fans. The favourable location and reasonable rates make up for the lack of a restaurant or pool. ②.

La Panache Guesthouse

Map 1, F2. Cas-en-Bas Road ℂ450-0765, fax 450-0453.

Run by the flamboyant Henry Augustin and famous for its weekly family-style West Indian dinners (see p.188), this is one of the area's best deals. Scattered on a hill with views west to Gros Islet, the seven colourful rooms all have private baths, mosquito nets and fans. There's a photograph-festooned restaurant, a gazebo-style lounge with TV and books to borrow, and Cas-en-Bas beach is only around 1500m to the east. ②.

Nelson's Furnished Apartments

Map 1, F2. Cas-en-Bas Road ℂ450-8275.

Mr Nelson's six apartments are not deluxe, but they have full kitchens, private baths and fans. Hot water is available, usually in the evenings. The location on the road to Cas-en-Bas is good for exploring the north end of the island and, if you've got a 4WD, the beaches on the east coast. ②.

R&R

Map 1, F2. Castries–Gros Islet Highway, Massade ℂ450-8689, fax 450-8134.

Twenty rooms, some with kitchens, on the east side of the busy Castries–Gros Islet Highway, convenient for exploring Rodney Bay, but a bit noisy. You can watch TV in a small common room and there's an inexpensive pizza joint below. ②.

CAP ESTATE

LeSPORT

Map 1, F1. Castries–Gros Islet Highway ℂ450-8551, fax 450-0368; in US ℂ1-800/544-2883.

A world-class, all-inclusive spa centre with a decent beach but a slightly snooty atmosphere. The emphasis is on pampering; everything from Swedish massage to salt loofah rubs, reflexology and seaweed wraps are included in the rates, as are watersports, aerobics, golf lessons, T'ai Chi, archery and fencing. ⑦.

Odyssey St Lucia

Map 1, F1. Castries–Gros Islet Highway, Anse Bécune
ℂ450-0551, fax 452-0281; in US ℂ1-800/777-1250.
A big, unpretentious and kid-friendly all-inclusive. Rooms are good value and comfortable, though not luxurious (the beachside Ocean View block is best); some have living rooms with pull-out beds, others fans but no a/c. The main 375-seat dining room is reminiscent of a school cafeteria, but there are other eating places. Smuggler's Cove is within walking distance, and there's another good private beach for watersports. Tennis at the resort's club is included. ⑥.

SOUFRIÈRE AND THE WEST COAST

Staying along the west coast between Castries and Soufrière is ideal if you want to get away from heavily trafficked tourist areas and relax in some of the finest resorts and guesthouses on the island. The beaches are inviting and uncrowded, and the limited number of accommodation choices (the vast majority in **Marigot Bay** or **Soufrière)** tend to be less resort-like than those further north. Staying in peaceful Marigot isn't a cheap option, but there are several budget hotels and guesthouses in downtown Soufrière, as well as luxurious resorts on its out-skirts. Public transport north and south of Soufrière is frequent; if you're travelling to Castries, the fastest route is via Vieux Fort, where you switch buses for the Castries leg (see p.112).

MARIGOT BAY

Club Mariner Hotel

Map 1, D6. ℂ451-4357, fax 451-4353; in US ℂ1-800/437-7880.
Attached to the service marina of the Caribbean's largest boat

charter outfit and, unsurprisingly, popular amongst yachties awaiting their crafts. The sixteen cottages are comfortable, and there's a pool, a well-regarded restaurant and watersports facilities. ④.

Inn on the Bay

Map 1, D6. ℂ451-4260, fax 451-4264.
Set 90m up on a hillside at the south side of the bay, this squeaky clean, four-room inn exudes romance. It's a quiet, slow-paced getaway – you feel like you're on top of the world looking down. Rooms overlook the deck and pool, and the sea breeze wafting up the hill renders a/c unnecessary and discourages mosquitoes. Breakfast is included, and the owners will prepare dinner twice per week – you eat on your porch overlooking the bay below. ④.

Marigot Beach Club

Map 1, D6. ℂ451-4974, fax 451-4973.
Ensconced on the north side of the bay and a couple of minutes from the road's end by water taxi, the location has long been the main draw; the open-air restaurant is named *Doolittle's* after the Rex Harrison movie filmed here in the 1960s. The 24 rooms are brimming with amenities, and the pool, beach, watersports and shops will keep you busy. ④.

Sea Horse Inn

Map 1, D6. ℂ451-4436, fax 451-4872.
Reached via water taxi from the docks, this elegant but simple getaway on the north side of the bay is set in a 1920s stone house which affords postcard-perfect views of the bay. The eight rooms have mosquito nets, overhead fans and en-suite bathrooms. Guests can use the kitchen by the breezy public room/restaurant, and you can cool off at the small pool. Rates include breakfast. ③.

ACCOMMODATION: MARIGOT BAY

Anse Chastanet

Map 5, A1. Anse Chastanet ©459-7000, fax 459-7700; in US ©1-800/223-1108, in UK ©0800/894-4220.

Genteel, old-style resort spread over a hill above Soufrière's nicest beach. Reminiscent of luxurious treehouses (some have branches growing through the floors), the large, airy rooms afford good ocean or mountain views and have floor-to-ceiling louvred walls, an open porch, mosquito nets and fan. The restaurant, bar, shops, spa and some rooms are on the beach, 100 steps below reception and the breakfast terrace. There's a great in-house diving outfit, and the beach is good for snorkelling. ⑦.

Cascara Guest House

Map 5, D6. Upper Church Street, Soufrière ©459-7581.

A slightly run-down but inexpensive guesthouse in the hills south of town on the road to Choiseul. Rooms downstairs share a shower and bath, and others upstairs share baths and a common kitchen. The draw is the price rather than the rooms. ①.

Chez Camille

Map 5, C4. Church Street and Boulevard Street, Soufrière ©459-5379.

Camilla's restaurant on Bridge Street is the contact for these two downtown guesthouses, both called *Chez Camille* and separated by a couple of blocks. Rooms are cosy, bright and secure with fans and mosquito nets; most share cold-water bathrooms. Each location has a small common room with a TV. No credit cards. ②.

Claudina's Guesthouse

Map 5, C5. 28 Bay Street, Soufrière ©459-7567.

Four rustic rooms near the waterfront, simply furnished with fans, double beds and mosquito nets. Guests share two shower/toilet units at the walled-in back patio, and can also use the common kitchen. As the room walls stop about two feet short of the ceiling, it's not ideal if you're seeking privacy. No credit cards. ②.

Jalousie Hilton Resort and Spa

Map 1, B10. Anse des Pitons ℂ459-7666, fax 459-7667; in US ℂ1-800/445-8667.

Well-run, cushy and enviably located slap between the Pitons, overlooking the quiet bay and a beach recently enhanced by US$1 million worth of pristine white sand imported from Guyana. Scattered throughout the 325-acre site, the rooms and villas are lavishly equipped with everything from robes and slippers to plunge pools. Amenities include several excellent bars and restaurants (the formal *Plantation Room* features haute cuisine), a hillside spa, fitness centre, watersports, shops, tennis, basketball, a putting green, and a water taxi service into town. Rooms ⑥, villas ⑦.

Hummingbird Beach Resort

Map 5, A1. Anse Chastanet Road ℂ459-7232 or 459-7492, fax 459-7033.

Pleasant, moderately priced inn on the north side of the beach, with a great restaurant. Furnished with reproduction plantation antiques (some have four-poster beds), rooms have overhead fans, mosquito nets and louvred windows. There's also a cottage across the road that sleeps four. The beach here is not great, but there is a pool. Rooms ②, cottage ④.

La Haut Plantation Resort

Map 5, C1. Castries–Soufrière Road ℂ459-7008, fax 454-9463.

Set in an old plantation house a couple of kilometres north of town, the five rooms are ample and comfortable rather than luxurious, with kitchenettes, ceiling fans, and expansive

views of the hills and Pitons. The restaurant and bar are
excellent. ②.

La Mirage Guesthouse

Map 5, C4. 14 Church Street, Soufrière ℂ & fax 459-7010.
Owner John Lamontagne worked as a chef in London for
nearly 40 years before returning home and opening the
Le Mirage guesthouse and restaurant in 1998. The four rooms
are clean and basic but comfortable and good value with en-
suite, hot-water bathrooms, a mini-fridge and a balcony
overlooking Church Street. No credit cards. ②.

Ladera Resort

Map 5, F7. Soufrière–Vieux Fort Road ℂ459-7323, fax 459-5156;
in US ℂ1-800/738-4752.
Views are a key element to this unusual hillside resort, which
looks down 300m over the *Jalousie Hilton*, the Pitons and the
bay. Deliberately open to the elements, rooms are without a
back wall in order to maximize both the views and the sense
of being at one with nature; night-time tree-frog concertos
are deafening. Built mostly of stone with carved wood
furnishings, each has mosquito nets, plunge pool or hot tub
and a large step-in shower. The restaurant is one of the
island's finest, and there's a pool, plus a shuttle service to
nearby beaches. ⑦.

Still Plantation Beach Resort

Map 5, A1. Anse Chastanet Road ℂ459-5179 or 459 7261,
fax 459-7301.
This small inn on the north side of town has bright upstairs
rooms cooled by overhead fans and the sea breeze; some have
kitchens and TV, all have mosquito nets and are linked by a
common balcony above the popular beachside restaurant and
bar. The beach is nearby, but it's not the island's best. ②,
③ with kitchen.

Still Plantation

Map 5, G3. Fond St Jacques Road ©459-5179 or 459-7261, fax 459-7301.

Out on the road to Fond St Jacques, near the turnoff for the Diamond Waterfall, is a sprawling and rather lifeless hotel on a 400-acre estate, with fourteen modern, fan-cooled studios and apartments; the latter have kitchens. There's a restaurant, pool, and bar on site, and beach shuttles are complimentary. ②, ④ with kitchen.

Stonefield Estate

Map 5, C7. Soufrière–Vieux Fort Road ©459-7037 or 453-0777, fax 459-5550.

Set in a working cacao plantation littered with the remains of nineteenth-century equipment, these ten spacious villas (one can sleep six) have kitchens, overhead fans, porches with hammocks and unscreened louvred widows. The larger villas seem half-decorated and curiously empty; smaller, one-bedroom units (there are four) are the best bets. A pool, restaurant and bar are on site, and beach shuttles are free. ⑦.

Sunset Guesthouse

Map 5, B3. Corner of Palmiste and Cemetery roads, Soufrière © & fax 459-7100.

Six basic rooms on the north side of town, two with en-suite baths and a/c, four with shared baths and fan. Balconies hang over the street with views to the fire station, and the location is good for exploring town. The owners run the inexpensive West Indian restaurant next door. ②.

THE SOUTH COAST

The area **south of Soufrière**, through the fishing villages of Choiseul and Laborie, is more residential than tourist-oriented and offers a relaxed alternative to the relentless activity of the northwest coast. Several excellent guesthouses can be found on or near the inviting beaches that line the coastal road from Soufrière to Vieux Fort. **Vieux Fort** itself also hosts several decent hotels and guesthouses, within easy reach of the airport.

Balenbouche Estate

Map 1, C13. Balenbouche Bay ℗455-1244, fax 455-1342.
Scattered with fruit trees, old water wheels by the river, Amerindian rock carvings and wandering farm animals, Uta Lawaetz's engaging but slightly run-down 150-acre plantation just south of Choiseul is a welcoming and friendly place. Anse Touloulou beach is a twelve-minute walk away, and the clean, cosy rooms are in the great house or two nearby cottages; some share baths, some have cold water only, some have kitchens. Meals available. ②, ④ with kitchen.

Beanfield Cottages

Map 1, F14. Beanfield, Vieux Fort ℗454-6260, fax 454-7436.
These 22 cottages on windswept Cloudnest Beach have seen much better days, but represent the best budget option in the area nonetheless. Each has two or three bedrooms, two baths and a kitchen. Expect some noise from the popular restaurant and nightclub on the grounds. No credit cards. ①.

Club Med

Map 1, F13. Beanfield, Vieux Fort ℗454-6546 or 454-6547, fax 454-9641; in US ℗1-800/258-2633.
Recently reopened after an expensive renovation, this 250-room resort is the biggest on the south coast, and is ensconced behind guarded gates that lend a somewhat unwelcoming feel. Rooms are adequately luxurious, there are pools, tennis courts and a restaurant on site, and some structured activities are laid on for kids. The beach is long and lovely, and watersports are available, though as the resort is only semi all-inclusive, you'll pay extra for sports such as scuba diving. ⑥.

Juliette's Lodge

Map 1, F14. Beanfield, Vieux Fort ℂ454-5300, fax 454-5305.
Conveniently close to Hewanorra International Airport and
popular amongst airline crews. Rooms are comfortable and
clean, and there's a sometimes harried restaurant serving basic
but hearty fare, and a pool; the beach is a few hundred yards
down the road. ③.

Miss Lucy's Mini Guesthouse

Map 1, C12. Choiseul ℂ459-3142, fax 459-3219.
Set on the main road at La Fargue, halfway between Soufrière
and Vieux Fort, and just outside Choiseul, this small white-
painted guesthouse has six basic rooms, all but one of which
share two shower and toilet units. Guests can use a common
kitchen and the sitting room has a TV. There's an average
beach within walking distance. No credit cards. ②.

Skyway Inn

Map 1, F14. Beanfield, Vieux Fort ℂ454-7111, fax 454-7116.
Your basic airport hotel, with comfortable, large rooms, a pool
that's usually dominated by airline crews, a bar popular with
locals, and a restaurant that's good for breakfast. The beach is a
couple of minutes away. ③.

THE EAST

There are only a couple of hotels between Vieux Fort and
Dennery. This is a rural and residential area characterized
by fishing communities and striking, often deserted bays.
However, there are a couple of nice spots to stay that make
convenient bases if you're planning on exploring the central
rainforests. North of Dennery, the coast is difficult to
access, and accommodation choices are virtually nil.

Fox Grove Inn

Map 1, G9. Mon Repose ℂ455-3271, fax 455-3800.

Located high in the hills several kilometres south of Dennery, with views of the popular Praslin Bay and Fregate Islands, this is a gem of a B&B and a good deal if you want to get away from the beach scene. The Swiss/St Lucian owners whip up a great lunch and offer horseback rides on nearby beaches and into the hills. Comfortable rooms are cooled by overhead fans. There's a swimming pool and a games room with pool table. ②.

Manje Domi

Map 1, F11. Desruisseaux ℂ455-0729.

Small guesthouse in the interior, about 13km from Vieux Fort; take the east-coast road toward Dennery, turn inland at the sign for Anse Ger and proceed up the hill for about a kilometre. The Creole name means "Eat, Sleep," which pretty well sums it up. The restaurant has a good reputation, and it's a fine location to get away from crowds and explore the Des Cartiers Rainforest trails. ②.

Eating and drinking

T hough St Lucia's **restaurant scene** is dominated by small, reasonably priced eateries with few pretensions, there are a few upmarket restaurants offering haute cuisine, and you're unlikely to be disappointed by them. Castries hosts a fair number of excellent eateries, including the popular Castries Central Market stalls (proof of the old adage that the best places to eat are where the locals go), but the majority of St Lucia's restaurants are clustered around the tourist areas.

A fair range of **cooking styles** splash the island's culinary map, but by far the most prevalent – and the best – is known, like the St Lucian language, as **Creole**. Heavily reliant on fresh seafood, fruits and exotic vegetables, Creole dishes reflect the history of the island's diverse population, mixing the spicy, tomato-based sauces and starchy carbohydrates of African-derived cooking with a flair for inventive garnishes, a throwback from years of French dominance (common Creole dishes and ingredients are listed in the glossary on pp.176–77). Other options include **Asian**, **French**, **Mexican**, **English** and **American Nouveau** styles, while **fast food** exists in the form of basic burgers and barbecue, imported *KFC* or local pizza joints such as *Pizza! Pizza!* and *Peppino's*.

Of available alcoholic **drinks**, the favourite local tipple is the light and rather mild Piton **beer**, brewed in Vieux Fort and dubbed the "Mystic Mountain Brew". A variation called Piton shandy borrows from the British tradition by mixing beer with something sweet, in this case ginger ale. St Lucia has also followed Caribbean tradition by producing some fine **rums**. St Lucia Distillers produces several brands; among the best are Old Fort Reserve, a smooth dark variety, and Denros, a strong white rum. Also on the shelves are Bounty (the island's best seller for its even taste), Five Blondes, and Crystal brands. Those with a sweet tooth will appreciate several interesting rum **liqueurs**, among them La Belle Creole Black Satin coffee liqueur and Ti Tasse coffee rum liqueur, often mixed in exotic drinks or served after dinner with desserts and coffee. **Soft drinks** such as Pepsi are both imported and bottled locally, and distilled water is widely available. For a cheap and healthy alternative, try **coconut water**. Drunk straight from the opened husk of a green nut, the juice is naturally sterilized and rich in potassium and other minerals. You'll find vendors at the markets and roadside stands throughout the island.

Restaurant prices and payment

The restaurants reviewed in this chapter have been graded **inexpensive** (US$10 or less), **moderate** (US$11–20), **expensive** (US$21–30) and **very expensive** (over US$30), based on the average price of a main meal excluding drinks and service charge.

Most restaurants in the tourist areas will accept **credit cards**, but small mom-and-pop operations like the barbecue pits at the Gros Islet street party probably won't. Restaurants generally tack on a ten percent **service charge** to your bill, meant to be a tip. Feel free to add extra if you feel the service warrants it – remember, the unfortunate truth is that some restaurants do not pass on the service charge to their staff.

St Lucian food glossary

accra deep-fried salted cod fritter

boudin spicy blood sausage

breadfruit called *bwape* in Creole, these starchy, bland fruits grow on trees and are eaten fried or boiled

brochette skewered and barbecued meats and vegetables

callaloo leafy green vegetable that looks and tastes like spinach and is often used to make soup

carambola a sweet, star-shaped fruit

chataigne breadfruit-like fruit with large seeds, prepared as a vegetable side dish

christophene vegetable with white, watery flesh, eaten boiled or sauteed

colombo meat, usually goat, lamb or chicken, in a spicy curry sauce

dasheen starchy root vegetable

fig green or ripe bananas

float deep-fried semi-sweet dough, sort of a St Lucian doughnut, so-named because it floats when fried; it's eaten as a snack on its own or as a side dish with fish

jerk method of seasoning meat, usually chicken, pork, or fish, with a multispice mixture heavy on pepper and pimento, which is then roasted slowly over wood or charcoal

koko coconut in Creole

lambi conch

love apple tropical fruit with pulpy, sweet flesh

mago mango in Creole

papaya, pawpaw, papay in Creole; large orange or yellow fruit high in both vitamins and an enzyme used as a meat tenderizer

pepperpot soup spicy soup of beef and callaloo

plantain a larger, blander member of the banana family that

turns from savoury to sweet as it ripens, and is eaten fried or
boiled at either stage

roti flat, baked unleavened bread wrapped around a mix of
curried vegetables or meat

saltfish salted cod

saltfish and green fig St Lucia's national dish of reconstituted,
fried saltfish with cooked green banana

soursop a large, green, rough-skinned fruit that yields white,
pulpy and sweet, not sour, flesh

sweetsop smaller version of a soursop

tamarind tropical tree that bears the pod from which acidic,
sour fruit is eaten, also used to make relish-like syrups, candy
and drinks

titiri small fish, deep-fried and eaten whole

ugli descriptive name of a hybrid citrus fruit, a cross between a
grapefruit and tangerine, developed in Jamaica in the early
1900s

Like most of St Lucia's shops and businesses, many of the
island's restaurants are closed on Sundays, when your best
bet is likely to be hotel restaurants. Also note that during
the off-season, **opening hours** and days might change, and
some restaurants close for up to a month at a time. While
we've given opening hours for most establishments, many
will stay open as long as they have custom; it's best to call
ahead for **reservations**, particularly in the high season –
some restaurants will even transport you to and from your
hotel at no extra cost.

CASTRIES

There's a fair selection of places to eat downtown, which are
good for grabbing a quick bite while shopping or sightseeing.

You'll probably be lunching with local businesspeople on their break, a situation that holds the downtown eateries to high standards and uninflated prices. For a more formal meal, head into the surrounding hills, where stunning views accentuate the experience.

Castries Central Market

Map 2, E4. Jeremie Street ✆453-6580.
Daily 6am–5pm. Inexpensive.

Market vendors, shoppers and local businesspeople flock to eat breakfast or lunch at these dozen or so restaurant stalls in a small, crowded alleyway behind the market. Taken at unadorned plastic tables, the servings of seafood, rotis, rice and beans or meat and dumplings are hearty and delicious. Most stalls don't accept credit cards.

Creole House

Map 2, F6. Brazil Street ✆452-3238.
Daily 8am–midnight. Moderate.

Set two blocks east of Derek Walcott Square in a colourful gingerbread building that survived the fires of the early nineteenth century. Serves savoury traditional Creole fare such as callaloo soup and codfish accras.

Naked Virgin

Map 1, E4. Marchand Road ✆452-5594.
Daily: lunch & dinner. Moderate.

Creole specialities, including a famous Shrimp Creole, as well non-Creole chicken and seafood dishes. The "Naked Virgin" is a startling rum-punch drink which packs a mighty kick.

Peppino's Pizza

Map 2, D7. Upper Bridge Street ✆457-7466.
Daily: lunch & dinner. Inexpensive.

Good pizza, calzones, and some traditional Italian pasta dishes are the fare at this typical pizza-joint. There's another branch at the Gablewoods Mall north of town.

Rain

Map 2, D6. Brazil Street ✆457-7246 or 452-1515.
Mon–Sat 8am–11pm. Moderate.
One of the city's best restaurants, beautifully located on the second floor of a gingerbread town house opposite Derek Walcott Square; tables on the outside verandah are well worth reserving. The menu is eclectic and the dishes (Creole prawns, fish in peanut curry or grilled pork ribs) are well executed.

AROUND CASTRIES

Several very good restaurants – and a couple that rank amongst St Lucia's very best – are found around the Vigie Peninsula, Morne Fortune and the hills to the east of Castries. Catering to an upscale business community, they are renowned for innovative cuisine and a more sophisticated, urban ambience than you'll encounter elsewhere on the island. Popular with both tourists and local people, most are usually busy, so reservations are recommended. North of Castries, along the Castries–Gros Islet Highway, is the Choc Bay area, with several beachside restaurants and bars that are worth a visit for their relaxed, oceanside atmosphere and solid fare.

THE MORNE AND MORNE FORTUNE

Bon Appétit

Map 3, B8. Morne Road, Morne Fortune ✆452-2757.
Mon–Fri 11am–2pm & 6.30–9.30pm, Sat & Sun 6.30–9.30pm. Expensive.
Reservations are essential at this popular five-table restaurant in the Castries hills. House specialities are steaks and seafood, the

cuisine is international and French nouveau – smallish servings tastefully arranged and embellished with minimal amounts of heavy sauces – and the wine selection is as impressive as the views of the harbour below.

Green Parrot

Map 3, B8. The Morne ℂ452-3399 or 452-3167.
Daily 7am–late. Expensive.

Irascible chef Harry Edwards once cooked at the illustrious *Claridge's* hotel in London, but now he's content with presiding over restaurant floorshows and working a James Bond theme into the menu; try Beef Thunderballs a la Flambe or Steak Pussy Galore. Other dishes include roast duck in orange sauce or fish Creole, and the cooking is enhanced by views of Castries harbour. The restaurant will pay round-trip taxi fares for groups of four or more, and the one-way fare for parties of two.

San Antoine

Map 3, C7. The Morne ℂ452-4660.
Mon–Fri 11.30am–2.30pm & 6.30–10.30pm, Sat 6.30–10.30pm. Expensive.

Set in a restored plantation great house on The Morne, this is a good choice for an elegant night out, offering International staples such as steak stuffed with shrimp Béarnaise, lobster thermidor or grilled fish in peppercorn sauce, an extensive wine list and views to the town below. They'll provide taxis for parties of four or more.

VIGIE AND AROUND

Beach Facilities

Map 3, D5. Vigie Beach ℂ452-5494.
Mon–Sat 10am–2am. Inexpensive.

Small, dark and right on the beach at the east end of the airport runway, offering hearty and inexpensive local food with

no frills – mutton stew, fried fish, curried chicken etc.
Things liven up at night with occasional live or canned music.
No credit cards.

D's

Map 3, E4. Edgewater Beach Club, Vigie Beach ✆453-7931.
Mon–Sat 11am–11pm. Moderate.

Beachside bistro with a touch of elegance, specializing in
Creole seafood dishes. The waterside setting is appealing, and
the food won't disappoint either.

Coal Pot

Map 3, B5. Vigie Marina, Vigie ✆452-5566.
Mon–Fri noon–2pm & 7–9pm, Sat 7–9pm.
Expensive–very expensive.

One of the island's busiest restaurants – dinner reservations are
essential. The New World cuisine is French-influenced,
decorative and pricey, but the seafood is fresh and the salads are
recommended. Directly on the water's edge, the dark interior
is embellished with local artwork; this is a perfect place for a
special night out.

Gablewoods Mall

Map 3, F3. Sunny Acres, no phone.
Mon–Sat 9am–7pm. Moderate.

The mall's food court offers Mexican dishes at *El Burrito*,
southeast Asian cuisine at *Miss Saigon*, and pizza/Italian food
at *Peppino's*. Also in the mall is the small, art-adorned *Tiggis*,
serving espresso, cappuccino, sandwiches, rotis, macaroni pie
and sweet pastries.

Jimmie's

Map 3, C6. Vigie Marina ✆452-2142.
Daily 9am–late. Moderate.

A warm, personal bar and restaurant that's big on hearty food and low on showy veneer. The restaurant sits above the marina, and the fare is fresh, home-style West Indian with an emphasis on seafood – try the large seafood platter with samplings of the day's catch.

Ti Cafe

Map 2, B2. Pointe Seraphine shopping complex, no phone.
Mon–Fri 9am–5pm, Sat 9am–2pm. Inexpensive.
Small kiosk in the middle of the duty-free mall that offers a relaxing break from the rigours of credit-card crunching. Fresh juices, coffee, espresso, cappuccino and light snacks are taken at umbrella-covered tables.

Waves Beach Bar

Map 3, F3. Castries–Gros Islet Highway, Choc Bay ©451-3000.
Daily 10am–1am. Moderate.
Roadside/beachside joint serving standard bar fare: chicken wings, fish fingers, burgers, ribs and steaks. You won't come for fine dining, but for access to the watersports facilities, showers and the beach (a fence provides unattractive if necessary solitude). Daytime entertainment includes karaoke (Tues) and family barbecues with live music (Sun).

GROS ISLET AND THE NORTH

Back-to-back restaurants in the busy "Golden Mile" north of Castries provide a staggering number of choices. Beachside eateries along Reduit Beach offer dining with sea breezes, and Rodney Bay as a whole seems to have more restaurants per square mile than anywhere else on the island, most clustered around the intersection of the Castries–Gros Islet highway and Reduit Beach Road. During the Friday night street party in Gros Islet, restaurateurs and vendors set up roadside barbecues and sell roasted chicken, fish or meats, as well as cold beers to wash it down – check *Hector's,*

Cecilia's and *Nigels Bar* for inexpensive and delicious barbecue. North of Gros Islet, the restaurants thin out a bit, but a number of vendors set up in front of the entrance to Pigeon Point and at the causeway beach, selling tasty barbecued chicken, roasted vegetables and floats. East of Gros Islet, on the road to Cas-en-Bas, *La Panache* is a fun experience, and boasts one of the area's more authentic Creole menus.

RODNEY BAY

Burger Park and The Bistro
Map 4, G8. Rodney Bay Marina ✆452-9494.
Burger Park 11am–10pm, closed Thurs;
The Bistro 5–10pm, closed Thurs. Inexpensive–moderate.
A rather anomalous combination of burger joint, alfresco restaurant, playground and miniature golf course that makes a good bet for families – the half-pound burgers, fish and chips, foot-long hot dogs and onion rings are good, cheap and greasy. On the waterfront and open for dinner only, *The Bistro* is more upscale, with steak-and-kidney pies, grilled duck breast and snapper in potato crust. No credit cards at *Burger Park*.

Capone's
Map 4, E8. ✆452-0284.
Dining room Tues–Sun 6.30–11pm,
La Piazza Tues–Sun 11am–midnight. Moderate–expensive.
One of the string of restaurants in Rodney Bay's eating epicentre, serving somewhat overrated and mundane Italian dinners in a gangster-inspired ambience – drinks include a good-sized Mafia Mai Tai. The small *La Piazza* pizzeria next door serves lunch, mostly pizzas and salads.

Charthouse
Map 4, E8. Rodney Bay Marina ✆452-8115.
Mon–Sat 5–11pm. Expensive.

Steaks and ribs are the specialities, and as they're cooked better here than anywhere on the island, reservations are necessary. The dark-wood, marina-side restaurant (reserve seats on the waterside deck) also serves seafood and Creole dishes.

Top it off with a Cuban cigar, on sale at the restaurant.

La Creole

Map 4, G8. Rodney Bay Marina ℂ450-0022.
Daily 11.30am–10pm. Moderate–expensive.

Commanding an excellent position on the marina and specializing, unsurprisingly, in Creole dishes with the emphasis on seafood. You can even pick your lobster from the restaurant aquarium if you've got the nerve. For dessert, try the homemade peanut ice cream. There's dancing every evening and occasional live music.

Eagles Inn

Map 4, F6. Reduit Beach Road ℂ452-0650.
Daily: lunch & dinner. Moderate.

A good lunch spot at the far end of the Reduit Beach Road, up against the Rodney Bay marina channel, specializing in grilled and barbecued seafood, chicken and ribs etc. The waterside setting is appealing, and you're just across the street from the beach.

Key Largo

Map 4, G8. Castries–Gros Islet Highway ℂ452-0282.
Daily 9am–11pm. Moderate.

Casual pizza place on the east side of the Castries–Gros Islet Highway, across from the marina, serving the best pizza on the island, freshly cooked in a wood-fired brick oven.

The Lime

Map 4, E8. ℂ452-0282.
Lunch & dinner, closed Tues. Moderate.

"Liming" is West Indian slang for "hanging out", and this is one of Rodney Bay's more popular spots to do just that. The eclectic menu is a mix of steaks and seafood, you can sit inside or alfresco on the patio next to the road, and the guitar player will sing you through dinner and drinks.

Mel's Olde English Pub

Map 4, E9. ✆452-0363.
Daily 12.30pm–late. Moderate.
Unassuming restaurant serving hearty traditional English fare such as kidney pies, hand-cut chips and boiled meat as well as good imported beer alongside the local brews. The popular Sunday brunch is a feast: roast beef, Yorkshire pudding and all the trimmings. Turn into Rodney Bay at the main entrance, then head left past the *Islander Hotel*.

Memories of Hong Kong

Map 4, E9. ✆452-8218.
Mon–Sat 5pm–late. Moderate.
Traditional and very good Cantonese and Asian delicacies are the main fare here, where the clattering kitchen is open to the restaurant. To find it, turn into Rodney Bay at the main entrance; it's near *Mel's Olde English Pub* and the *Islander Hotel*.

Miss Saigon

Map 4, E8. ✆452-0580.
Daily 5pm–midnight. Moderate.
Owner Myrna Esquillo hails from the Philippines, and her fine, if small, eatery on a side street near the main Rodney Bay drag serves delicate and tasty Southeast Asian cuisine; try the king prawns in Thai green curry sauce, or the creamy lamb korma. The Asian dishes are vastly preferable to the standard grilled ribs, fish and steaks that are also on offer. Seating is inside or alfresco.

EATING AND DRINKING: RODNEY BAY

Mortar & Pestle

Map 4, E8. *Harmony Marina Suites* ✆452-8756.
Daily 7.30am–midnight. Moderate–expensive.
One of the first restaurants in the area, and still one of the finest with a great location right on the water. The theme is engaging – dishes from various Caribbean islands are offered, from Antigua conch and Martinique-style fish to Trinidad calypso chicken and ginger pork from St Vincent. There is live entertainment each Tuesday, Thursday and Sunday.

Natasha's Café

Map 4, G7. Rodney Bay Marina ✆452-0446.
Daily 7am–midnight. Inexpensive.
Set on a patio above the Royal Bank building in the marina complex, this is a basic sandwiches and cold beer sort of place. But the marina setting is relaxing and pretty, and *Natasha's* makes a nice breakfast spot for staples such as muffins, pastries, omelettes and French toast.

Pizza! Pizza!

Map 4, E8. ✆452-8282.
Mon, Tues, Thurs & Sun 11am–midnight,
Wed, Fri & Sat 11am–2am. Inexpensive.
The owners have sunk some money – but not a lot – into this hallway-sized pizza joint-cum-takeaway. It's on the bottom floor of the building that houses *Snooty Agouti*, with the only seating outside in a small garden and playground by the marina. The deep-dish pizza is a good option.

Razmataz

Map 4, E7. Reduit Beach Road ✆452-9800.
4pm–late, closed Thurs. Moderate.
The best Indian restaurant on the island, across the street from the *Royal St Lucian Hotel* at Reduit Beach. Specialities are

spicy vindaloo (hot sauce), korma (cream and coconut sauce) and rogan josh (spicy sauce with cashews and garlic), all prepared with tandoori (grilled) chicken, lamb or beef – there are plenty of non-meat options as well, plus occasional live music.

Snooty Agouti

Map 4, E8. ℗452-0321.
Inexpensive.
Bizarrely reminiscent of a colourful Dennis Hopper movie set, but the café food is New Wavesque and savoury: vegetarian lasagne, twice-baked potatoes with cheese and broccoli, moussaka and exotic sandwiches. Coffees and desserts are not to be missed. This is a good breakfast stop (no breakfast Sunday in the slow season), you can shop or browse in the art gallery and there's live jazz most Thursday and Sunday evenings.

Spinnakers

Map 4, E7. Reduit Beach ℗452-8491.
Daily 9am–11pm. Moderate.
Appealing beach bar and restaurant serving an international mix of steaks, grilled seafood, and lobster that's more upscale than you'd expect for a beach bar. The setting is hard to beat, especially at sunset.

Triangle Pub

Map 4, E8. ℗452-0334.
Daily 8am–late. Inexpensive.
The streetside *Triangle* is the best beach grill in town, and will happily barbecue everything but your socks. But they do it well, with all the trimmings, and also provide music – steel bands on Tuesday, other bands on weekends – as well as organizing the occasional karaoke night. No credit cards.

GROS ISLET AND AROUND

Coco's

Map 4, E6. Coral Avenue and Marina Road, Gros Islet ℗450-0510.
Daily 7am–11pm. Inexpensive–moderate.

Set in a bamboo shack on the Gros Islet side of the Rodney
Bay marina, this small Creole restaurant serves decent, inexpensive seafood. No culinary awards but a good place to relax
at lunchtime. No credit cards.

La Panache

Map 1, F2. Cas-en-Bas Road ℗450-0765.
No set hours. Moderate.

Twice a week, Henry Augustin lays on one of the area's best
dining experiences at his friendly guesthouse; an informal,
five-course feast of West Indian food at its finest. The menu is
built around fresh fish, poultry and seasonally available market
veggies, and dishes are passed around family-style, elbows and
all. Call ahead to reserve a place.

Laurel's

Map 1, E2. Bois d'Orange ℗452-8547.
Mon–Sat 9am–1am. Moderate.

Turn toward the coast at the signs for the *Orange Grove Hotel*
and you'll see this small, no-frills Creole restaurant set in a
house. Seating is on the lawn or under a canopy on the ground
floor. Nicely cooked and served in lavish portions, dishes
include green figs and saltfish, lambi, fish Creole and garlic
shrimp.

CAP ESTATE AND AROUND

Great House

Map 4, F1. Castries–Gros Islet Highway, Cap Estate ℗450-0450.
Tues–Sun 4.30–10pm. Expensive.

Fine dining (afternoon tea and dinner only) in a 235-year-old stone plantation house overlooking Bécune Bay, with seating inside or on the stone patio. The cuisine is West Indian and French – try the lamb with garlic and rosemary – and the four-course set menu (around US$40) offers excellent value. Adjacent is the Derek Walcott amphitheatre, where you can see occasional works by the man himself before or after dinner, depending upon schedules.

Jambe de Bois

Map 4, A3. Pigeon Island ℘450-8166.
Daily 9am–5pm. Inexpensive.

The legendary one-legged pirate François Leclerc – *jambe de bois* means "wooden leg" – who made Pigeon Point his home never ate in this café, but he didn't miss much. The food is uninspired, but it's a pleasant setting by the sea inside the Pigeon Island complex and a good place to cool off; Creole shrimp and chicken, fish and chips, burgers and sandwiches are all served.

SOUFRIÈRE AND THE WEST COAST

The coast road south of Castries hosts a small number of good-value eateries, and Soufrière holds its own against the tourism strongholds of the northwest, with a wealth of eating places ranging from small cafés to more elegant restaurants for relaxed evening dining. Some of the hotels also offer wide-ranging evening menus and comfortable beachside restaurants for lunching during the day.

MARIGOT BAY

Chateau Mygo

Map 1, D6. Marigot Bay Road ℘451-4772.
Daily 7am–11pm. Moderate.

Appealing, simple little restaurant at the end of the Marigot Bay road just before the water taxi dock. Serving three meals per day, with seating upstairs (inside and on the patio) and downstairs; lunch and dinner specialities are grilled fish, Mama Shield's Creole Chicken and conch in a nutmeg curry sauce.

Hurricane Hole

Map 1, D6. *Club Mariner Hotel* ©451-4357.
Daily 8am–10pm. Moderate.
Pleasant hotel restaurant overlooking the yacht marina and bay. The tasty cuisine is overwhelmingly Creole – try the juicy mahi-mahi.

JJ's

Map 1, D6. Marigot Bay Road ©451-4076.
Daily 10am–late. Moderate.
The diminutive *JJ's* is on your left at the top of the hill just before the road descends into Marigot Bay. The servings of simple Creole food are generous, and the restaurant hosts live bands and other entertainment occasionally.

SOUFRIÈRE

Anse Chastanet

Map 5, A1. Anse Chastanet ©459-7354.
Daily: lunch & dinner. Moderate–expensive.
This beachside in-hotel bar and restaurant serves fine West Indian and international dishes, and their weekly barbecue buffet is one of the best and most elaborate meals of any available in Soufrière. If you're not driving, it's reachable via water taxi from the Soufrière waterfront (around EC$25 round-trip).

Bang

Map 5, E7. Anse des Pitons ©459-7864.
Daily noon–midnight. Moderate.

Right on the water at the south end of the *Jalousie Hilton* resort, reachable via water taxi from town (EC\$38 round-trip, per person), serving spicy, Jamaican jerk-style barbecued fish, chicken and other meats.

Camilla's

Map 5, B4. 7 Bridge Street ✆459-5379.
Daily 8am–midnight. Inexpensive.
A clean, bright place just a block from the waterfront, with two tables on a small, second-floor verandah overlooking the street. Vegetarian dishes such as vegetable rotis are on offer, as well as Creole-style fish, lamb, pork and conch. Breakfast is Creole fare such as saltfish and green fig, or eggs with bacon.

Dasheene

Map 5, F7. *Ladera Resort* ✆459-7323.
Daily 8–10am, 11am–2.30pm & 6.30pm–late. Expensive.
Chef Robbie Skeete's decoration as St Lucia's "Most Promising Chef" shows through in his cooking. The cuisine is an eclectic mix of West Indian, Oriental, Italian and vegetarian; traditional but artful, wholesome, and pretty damn good. The views of the Pitons and bay below are astonishing – come up for drinks before sunset and drift into dinner.

Fredo's

Map 5, C4. 10 Church Street ✆459-5220.
Mon–Fri 10am–7.30pm, Sat 10am–5pm. Inexpensive.
As there are only three tables, no decor to speak of and a menu limited to sandwiches, rotis, steak concoctions and seafood dishes, this is best for a quick snack. No credit cards.

Hummingbird Beach Resort

Map 5, A1. Anse Chastanet Road ✆459-7232.
Daily: breakfast, lunch & dinner. Moderate.
Lush gardens surround this small hotel restaurant on the beach,

which serves fresh juices, pastries, eggs and French toast for
breakfast, and sandwiches or fresh catch-of-the-day cooked
Creole-style for lunch and dinner. The fresh fruit juices are
worth trying, particularly the tart tamarind concoction. If you're
dining, you can use the hotel's small pool, beach and showers.

Jalousie Hilton Resort

Map 5, E7. Anse des Pitons ©459-7666.
Daily: breakfast, lunch & dinner. Moderate–very expensive.
There are three excellent choices within this glitzy resort;
housed in the main Great House, the refined *Plantation* serves
international cuisine (make reservations and dress up a bit),
while on the water at the south end of the resort, the *Pier* is a
more informal dinner option. On the beach, the *Bayside* serves
lighter meals for breakfast and lunch, and lays on the occasional
evening buffet with live entertainment.

La Mirage

Map 5, C4. 14 Church Street ©459-7010.
Mon–Sat 11.30am–10pm. Moderate.
An informal ground-floor restaurant serving vegetarian
specialities such as pasta and creative salads, as well as fish and
chips, roasted chicken and pizza, all of which are substantial
and sensibly priced.

Old Courthouse Restaurant

Map 5, C6. Soufrière waterfront ©459-5002.
Daily 8am–midnight. Moderate.
This bright lavender-painted building just north of the fish
market building is indeed an old courthouse, dating back to
1898 – the thick-doored bathrooms were the former cells.
Cuisine is solid and recommendable West Indian with Asian
twists – Creole conch and prawns, chicken in coconut curry
sauce and chicken tikka. With just nine tables, five overlooking
the water, reservations are essential.

EATING AND DRINKING: SOUFRIÈRE

Still Plantation Beach Resort

Map 5, A1. Anse Chastanet Road ©459-5179 or 459-7261.
Daily 7.30am–11pm. Moderate.

Served up under an ocean-facing canopy on the beach, the three daily meals are mostly Creole-based and spicy. Breakfast ranges from saltfish and green fig to omelette concoctions and fresh coffee, while lunch and dinner usually consist of pepper-pot soup, sweet-and-sour flying fish or freshwater prawns.

Sunset Guesthouse

Map 5, B3. Corner of Palmiste and Cemetery roads ©459-7100.
Daily 9am–11pm. Inexpensive.

More bar than restaurant, *Sunset* serves up inexpensive, basic West Indian breakfasts, lunches and dinners with no flourishes.

Talk to Me Cool Spot

Map 5, B1. Castries–Soufrière Road ©459-7437.
Mon–Sat 10am–3pm & 6–10pm. Inexpensive–moderate.

Perched on a hill, with tables on a patio overlooking the town and bay, the setting is as much of a draw as the cooking. Portions of substantial West Indian fare are garnished with fried plantains and carambola and the seafood comes recommended. To find it, turn off for the sign to Mago Plantation and it's on the left.

THE SOUTH

Though there's less choice than along the north and west coasts, the south has its share of good places to eat nonetheless. There are some reliable hotel restaurants near Hewanorra airport, and for snacks, try the beach bars along the Anse de Sables shoreline, or the tasty fried fish sold along the section of beach near to the *Chak Chak* restaurant. If you fancy some western-style fast food, there's a branch of *KFC* at JQ's Plaza in Vieux Fort.

Chak Chak

Map 1, F14. Beanfield, Vieux Fort ℭ454-6260.
Daily: lunch & dinner. Inexpensive–moderate.
Set amid a development of resort cottages, this is a popular
meeting spot for those heading to the adjacent *Zodiac*
nightclub, and the appealing prices attract patrons from nearby
hotels. Rickety tables are set in a dark and sparsely decorated
dining room or outside on the verandah, and the menu, based
around fresh fish, is serviceable. No credit cards.

Il Pirata

Map 1, F14. Vieux Fort ℭ454-6610.
Tues–Sun 9am–9.30pm. Moderate.
Dark Italian restaurant that isn't enhanced by a drab beachside
setting near to the crumbling remnants of an old dock. The
food, though, is a happy contrast; specialities include deep-
oven pizza, homemade pastas and a decent fish Milanese.

Juliette's Lodge

Map 1, F14. Beanfield, Vieux Fort ℭ454-5300.
Daily 7.30am–10pm. Moderate.
One of the better places to eat in Vieux Fort, and rather
besieged at times by large parties of airline crews. The basic
fare of fried fish, pasta and steaks is tasty and swiftly served.

The Reef

Map 1, F14. Anse de Sables ℭ454-7416.
Tues–Sat 10am–late. Inexpensive–moderate.
A basic beachside restaurant and bar serving standard fare of
beers, burgers, pizza and some West Indian dishes. The best
thing about it is its seashore location.

Sandy Beach Club

Map 1, F14. Anse de Sables ℭ454-7416.

Daily: lunch & dinner. Moderate.

On the sands at the southeast side of the airport, this beach bar and restaurant serves Creole dishes, burgers, sandwiches and exotic cocktails. It's one of the best places in Vieux Fort to eat, drink and relax by the ocean, though the opening hours are erratic – call ahead if you're planning on dinner.

THE EAST

The scenery along the **east coast** is certainly picturesque, but you won't find many worthy restaurants along the way. As the coastline north of Dennery is inaccessible in anything other than a 4WD, there are no established restaurants.

Fox Grove Inn

Map 1, G9. Mon Repose ©455-3271.
Daily 8am–10pm, 12.30–2.30pm & 7–10pm. Moderate–expensive.
About ten minutes' drive from Vieux Fort, this inland B&B is a relaxing spot for lunches or special dinners, and the dining room affords great views of the hills and the coastline as far as the Fregate Islands. Specials include both Creole and international dishes; try pan-fried dolphin, tuna in lime sauce or beef in pink pepper sauce.

Entertainment and nightlife

Though St Lucia isn't exactly the **nightlife** capital of the Caribbean, there's plenty to do after dark. Many hotels and restaurants in the west coast resort areas offer some sort of **live music** or **dancing** most nights of the week. Between Castries and Cap Estate, and particularly at Rodney Bay, there are numerous bars and restaurants where you can have a drink or a meal whilst listening to anything from a mellow jazz combo to the hotter licks of a reggae, calypso or steel pan band, or even traditional chak-chak groups and canned or live rock and roll. **Karaoke** is big at *Waves* in Choc Bay and the *Shamrock Pub* in Rodney Bay. Most pub-crawlers are a mix of young local people and tourists in search of dancing music, and if you're desperate for a dancefloor, head for the in-house **discos** of larger hotels, where DJs spin the latest from North America or Europe. For more sedate entertainment, seek out the few jazz and piano bars.

Many of the larger resort hotels also offer their own evening **entertainment**, and non-guests are welcome unless the property is all-inclusive. This often consists of seaside or poolside barbecues with steel bands or DJs playing, followed by those remarkably tacky **fire-eating** and **limbo dancing** shows that have become associated with the region despite the fact that fire-eating and limboing have nothing whatso-ever to do with Caribbean people. The performances are more of a carnival sideshow than a cultural indicator, but they're fun if you relish a spectacle. As the bulk of in-hotel entertainment takes place during the high season, it's best to call ahead to see what's on.

The best source of current entertainment **information** is local newspapers and the tourist publication *Tropical Traveller*. You can always call establishments directly – numbers are provided with listings on the following pages.

St Lucia hosts several **regular events**, and two of the biggest in the annual entertainment calendar are the **St Lucia Jazz Festival** in May – four days of jazz, R&B and world music – and July's **Carnival**, celebrated with music, dance and parades and preceded by weeks of calypso con-tests and feasts. Another event to look out for is the St Lucia National Trust's annual **Festival of Comedy** (℗452-5005), which showcases local comedy acts and theatre at the Cultural Centre in Castries and on Pigeon Island. A popular newcomer to the annual entertainment calendar is the early December **St Lucia Country Festival**, a four-day extrava-ganza held at Pigeon Island and the Derek Walcott Theatre at the *Great House* restaurant in Cap Estate. Past performers have included the Charlie Daniels Band, Neal McCoy and the late Tammy Wynette, and you can expect an enthusiastic audience; country music is strangely popular throughout the Caribbean. Tickets cost about US$30 for individual shows, or you can buy a pass for US$65, which admits you to all of the performances. Lastly, a rundown on the entertainment scene must include the island's liveliest weekly event, the **Gros Islet Street Party**, held in the open air each Friday night and quite possibly St Lucia's most visited, and most famous, night-time attraction.

ENTERTAINMENT AND NIGHTLIFE

ST LUCIA JAZZ FESTIVAL

Since it commenced in 1992, the annual **St Lucia Jazz Festival** has made a splash on the international scene and has attracted some of the jazz and R&B worlds' biggest names, including Grover Washington, Herbie Hancock, Nancy Wilson, Mary J. Blige, Earl Klugh, Wynton Marsalis, the Neville Brothers, steel pan artist Boogsie Sharp, Chick Corea, Stanley Clarke, Wayne Shorter and George Benson. The four-day event takes place in early or mid-May at several venues, the main ones being Pigeon Island and the Cultural Centre on the outskirts of Castries, while more intimate shows are held at an ever-changing array of resorts, nightclubs and venues around the country from Gros Islet to Vieux Fort. Many events are held outdoors at temporary stages erected for the shows, a wonderful way to combine the mellow energy of jazz with the relaxed tropical setting.

Some shows are free, such as the "Jazz in the Square" series held at Derek Walcott Square in Castries, but for most, you'll need to pay an entrance fee. **Tickets** for individual shows cost US$35–42, or you can buy a **pass** giving entry to all of the events for around US$230, good value if you plan to attend more than half a dozen concerts. The festival attracts thousands of tourists and music aficionados, and if you want to attend, it's advisable to make hotel and air reservations some months ahead to avoid disappointment.

The **festival Web site** (*www.stluciajazz.com*) has specific details about concerts and dates – you can even vote in advance for your favourite artist lineup and possibly win a free trip to the festival. General festival **information** is available from the tourist board in St Lucia (©452-5005) and from offices abroad (see pp.21–22).

St Lucian music

The roots of **St Lucian music** go back to the days when slaves fashioned instruments from whatever materials came to hand, and the repertoire of local **folk music** began with work and game songs and festival and dance songs. Known by the name of their principal instrument, early musical groups centred around a rhythm instrument called a *chak-chak*, often a tin or hollowed-out log filled with seeds, while the *tambou* (a wooden drum with a goatskin head) beat time and a small banjo called a *banjo bwa payé* provided melody. Several groups keep the traditions alive today, playing at national events such as Carnival, Independence Day celebrations and the La Rose and La Marguerite festivals. The **vocals** that accompany the music are often improvised, with audience members tossing in a line here and there; like calypso, *chak-chak* music offers social and political commentary, often mixed with ribald lyrics. If you want to take home some traditional St Lucian music, the "Musical Traditions of St Lucia" compilation is a good bet; it's available from the Folk Research Centre in Castries (①452-2279).

Modern popular music borrows from pan-Caribbean forms such as calypso, a favourite of Carnival, and soca, an upbeat dance music that mixes the storytelling tradition of calypso with the beat of America R&B. Reggae is also an island staple, and the frenetic sounds of *zouk*, a blend of funk, soca and African music which is popular in Martinique, Guadeloupe and other French islands, are guaranteed to fill the dance halls and discos.

....

**For a full list of St Lucia's festivals
and public holidays, see Basics, pp.46–49.**

....

ST LUCIAN MUSIC |

CARNIVAL

A round of dancing, street masquerading, competitive calypsoing, feasting and general partying, St Lucia's **Carnival** (called **Jounen Kwéyòl** in Patois) is one of the true showcases of the island's culture, with storytelling, folk dancing and traditional music such as chak-chak bands afforded as much prominence as the more contemporary Carnival melee of sequinned bikinis and thumping soca music. It's kid-friendly, too, with lots of children's costume parades and special events such as the Junior Carnival King and Queen contests.

While it might not seem so from the revelry that surrounds the event, Carnival has distinctly non-secular roots, having evolved amongst Catholics as a last fling before the austerity of Lent. In the Caribbean and further afield, the tradition gradually became Africanized, an opportunity for slaves to let loose and parody their owners with overblown costumes, music and dance traditions from their native lands. However, in an attempt to attract more tourists, and to avoid other popular Caribbean Carnivals (particularly that of Trinidad), the 1999 event was shifted from the original pre-Lenten dates to the second week of July. This may well be a permanent move, and it has generated a negative reaction from some locals. Many believe that the move to July will erase the true meaning of the festival and that Carnival will become just another tourist-oriented activity. Wary of the opposition, the government have declared the first July Carnival as a test run.

Carnival **information** is available from the tourist board in St Lucia (℅452-4094), and from offices abroad (see pp.21–22).

THEATRE

You can catch shows at various venues around the country, notably the **Derek Walcott Theatre**, a small open-air amphitheatre adjacent to the *Great House* restaurant in the Cap Estate hills (©450-0450). The theatre showcases local playwrights and actors, and the plays are well worth seeing for their insights into local culture, as well as for their literary value. Nobel Prize-winner Walcott is the inspiration for local writers, and he was instrumental in the theatre's development; his own work is also occasionally staged. Plays are in English or in Patois (not easy to understand), and range in theme and presentation from broad farce to serious drama. In general, St Lucians are not theatre-going folk, but the Castries crowd like to turn out for performances. Tickets start at about EC$10.

Also well worth checking out are the excellent singing and dancing performances by **Folk Research Centre** groups (©452-2279). The centre, on L'Anse Road in Castries' Morne Pleasant, presents their traditional, non-touristy productions year round, but the bulk are staged around Carnival time.

GROS ISLET STREET PARTY

Completely overtaking the village of Gros Islet, the popular Friday night **street party** (or **jump-up** as it's locally known) is the highlight of St Lucia's weekly nightlife schedule. The festivities are fairly self-explanatory: from around 10pm, the streets are packed with revellers dancing, drinking and feasting on barbecued food sold by hordes of enterprising vendors. Dauphine Street and its surrounds are closed to traffic, the bars are wide open, and the reggae, soca and calypso music blasts from all angles.

For more on the Gros Islet street party, see p.85.

It can be great fun, but a word of caution – of late, the party has started to attract vendors peddling marijuana and

GROS ISLET STREET PARTY

even sex alongside the fried chicken, and reports of crime suggest that it's sensible to leave valuables back at the hotel and bring with you only what you'll need to spend . Women should expect to be approached by aggressively interested (and sometimes overly persistent) men; for tips on how best to deal with this kind of attention, see Basics, p.42.

BARS AND LIVE MUSIC

The St Lucian **bar scene** is at its liveliest in Castries and Rodney Bay. Most drinking spots and hotel bars offer some sort of enticement to get people in, such as 5–7pm **happy hours** with two-for-one deals on drinks. **Ladies' nights** are also a draw, with free admission or reduced drinks prices for women. There are no set **licensing hours** in St Lucia, and most establishments will stay open as long as they have custom. Cover charges for the **live music** shows held in bars and pubs start at around US$5 per person.

CASTRIES AND AROUND

Beach Facilities
Map 3, D5. Vigie Beach ⌀452-5494.
This small, dark bar on Vigie beach offers cheap eats and the odd performance by live bands on weekends. With the waves lapping the shore, this is a pleasant place for a drink even after the sun goes down.

Rain
Map 2, D6. Brazil St, Castries ⌀457-7246 or 452-1515.
The period setting of this popular downtown restaurant in the old section of Castries makes it an appealing drinking spot, particularly for people-watching, as the porch overlooks Derek Walcott Square. Easy listening bands perform to a mix of locals and tourists most Friday and Saturday nights.

Waves Beach Bar

Map 3, F3. Choc Bay ℂ451-3000.

This beachside restaurant lays on occasional live music – look out for family nights and other theme evenings, as well as the regular Tuesday night karaoke songfest.

GROS ISLET AND THE NORTH

Indies

Map 4, G9. Rodney Bay ℂ452-0727.

Upscale in its own way – proper dress is required, meaning no beach wear – *Indies* puts on busy theme nights; the popular Wednesday "Beach Bash" provides drinks, music and round-trip transport from your hotel for one price (US$15). Friday and Saturday are often Ladies' Nights, when women get free drinks.

La Creole

Map 4, G8. Rodney Bay ℂ450-0022.

This popular seafood restaurant on the strip of land between the Castries–Gros Islet Highway and the Rodney Bay Marina has night-time salsa and disco dancing and occasional live music such as oldies bands or *zouk* from the French West Indies. Popular with tourists and locals alike.

The Lime

Map 4, E8. Rodney Bay ℂ452-0282.

Most nights, you'll hear a lone singer with guitar in the street-side courtyard of *The Lime* – clap for him once in a while, he's looking for it. The restaurant's next-door disco, *Late Lime*, is open Wednesday, Friday and Saturday for dancing to a wide range of live music, and sometimes hosts comedy acts. This is one of the island's hottest nightlife venues, likely to be crowded with young St Lucians and tourists feverishly dancing the night away.

BARS AND LIVE MUSIC: GROS ISLET AND THE NORTH

Razmataz

Map 4, E7. Rodney Bay ©452-9800.

The *Razmataz* serves East Indian fare and has live music on weekends as well as the occasional belly dancer.

Shamrock's Pub

Map 4, E8. Rodney Bay ©452-8725.

On the Rodney Bay waterfront, *Shamrock's* is a rocking place, and with something going on just about every night, it's bound to be crowded. On Monday you can get big pitchers of beer for about EC$15, Tuesday is Ladies' Night, when women get two-for-one drinks, and from Wednesday to Sunday there are theme nights with bands as well as the occasional karaoke evening. Also on hand are pool tables and table football games.

Snooty Agouti

Map 4, E8. Rodney Bay ©452-0321.

Snooty Agouti has a little bit of everything (see p.187), but on the entertainment front, there's live jazz on Tuesday and Sunday nights.

Triangle Pub

Map 4, E8. Rodney Bay ©452-0334.

Small barbecue next to *The Lime* which puts on live music every night, from reggae and steel bands to jazz. Great fun, and great food, too.

SOUFRIÈRE AND THE WEST COAST

JJ's

Map 1, D6. Marigot Bay Road ©451-4076.

On the road to the bay, *JJ's* runs a popular seafood night on Wednesday, with dancing to all sorts of music afterward, and a Friday Night Street Jam, smaller than but similar to the Gros Islet jump up. Speakers are set up outside of the restaurant, and there is some street mingling of locals and tourists from the bay hotels, with beers and eats from *JJ's*. It's a pleasant diversion if you'd rather avoid the more bombastic party at Gros Islet.

Club Zodiak

Map 1, F14. Beanfield Cottages, Beanfield, Vieux Fort ©454-6260. Set in the Beanfield Cottages complex, next to the *Chak Chak* restaurant, this makeshift disco is actually a small room with what appears to be aluminium foil plastered on the walls. There is live music at the weekends during the high season; otherwise, the DJs take over with loud reggae, rap and *zouk*. The crowd comprises mostly young St Lucians letting loose.

The Reef

Map 1, F14. Anse de Sables, Vieux Fort ©454-7416. Live music and dancing on the beach during high-season weekends for a predominantly young crowd of tourists, locals and students from a nearby medical school. During the off season, call to find out if there's anything happening.

Sport

With miles of easily accessible sandy beaches and the vast ocean never more than a couple of miles away, St Lucia is perfect for **watersports**. Larger resort hotels often have their own watersports facilities, usually **snorkelling**, **scuba diving**, **sea kayaking**, **wind-surfing** and **sailing** on small, single-sail one- or two-person Sunfish boats. Some places also have their own **yachts**, often catamarans, for sunset and snorkelling excursions, as well as fishing trips. Except at all-inclusives, non-guests can usually use in-hotel facilities – for a fee, of course.

If no watersports are on offer where you're staying and you don't want to use the facilities at other hotels, there are numerous privately run outfits at St Lucia's marinas and the more popular beaches. In the **north** of the island, the best places to start are the Vigie Marina in Castries and the Rodney Bay Marina near Rodney Bay town; the Moorings Marina at **Marigot Bay** is a good bet if you're staying in the area; and in the **south**, try the waterfront in Soufrière, where several fishing boats and excursion yachts dock. Beaches on the west coast are generally calm and safe for **swimming**, but some in the east have dangerous rough spots, easily recognizable by the crashing surf which often indicates strong undertows. Ask local advice, and go in only up to your knees if you're not a strong swimmer. The waters surrounding the island are pretty clean, but uncon-firmed reports suggest that Reduit Beach and Rodney Bay may harbour some **pollution**. In most cases, swimming in rivers and waterfalls is safe, though you should take your cue from locals. Try to swim upstream, as the closer a river gets to the coast, the more likely it is to be polluted.

There's plenty to do out of the water as well. Easily accessible **land-based sports** include **tennis**, **squash**, **golf** and **horseback riding**; larger hotels often have **gyms** as well – there are also a couple of privately run outfits in Gablewoods Mall. While many of the more sizeable hotels have tennis courts (and, again, allow non-guests to use them for a fee), there are also several public courts with good facilities – some of these also have resident pros who can provide lessons. St Lucia has one public golf course at Cap Estate, though it's likely to be crowded during week-ends in the busy winter season.

SCUBA DIVING

St Lucia's **diving** is not as highly regarded as the region's more pristine scuba environments, such as Saba or Bonaire. Visibility is generally fair, but rivers spilling into the ocean at places such as Soufrière and Vieux Fort bays can muddy the vistas. Still, many of the reefs – particularly in the south around the base of the Pitons – are excellent dive sites, and there are several submerged wrecks to explore.

If you've never tried scuba diving, it's easy to learn in St Lucia by taking a PADI (Professional Association of Diving Instructors) beginners' training course. Known as **resort courses**, these take you through the basics (usually in a swimming pool), before heading to the ocean for a super-vised dive of about forty feet (12m). Costs start at US$80. If you're interested (and have both the time and the money), more detailed certification programmes such as open water, advanced open water and refresher courses are available from various dive centres for US$200–450. These generally include daily dive fees, manuals, dive tables, a log book and certification processing fees, and sometimes equipment.

If you have **certification**, you should of course bring along your card as well as any pieces of equipment you'd rather not rent. Some operators include diving gear in their packages, so it's worth checking beforehand. If you're certified, **prices** start at about US$50 for a one-tank dive, with night dives costing from US$70. Packages for multiple dives start at US$120 for four dives over two days, and go up to as much as US$280 for ten dives in five days. If you're a serious enthusiast, it might be worth looking into packages offered by hotels such as *Anse Chastanet* or the *Marigot Beach Club*, which bundle flights, accommodation and a specified number of dives at ostensibly discounted rates – however, deals vary, and it's worth checking the specifics before you book.

SNORKELLING

Snorkelling is particularly good around the island's south-western fringes, where the **Soufrière Marine Management Area** (see p.100) hugs the shoreline for nearly seven miles from Anse L'Ivrogne south of Gros Piton to Anse Jambon, just north of Anse Chastanet. The reefs here are pristine by most standards, and the area is set aside as a protected area for fishing and recreational use; the nominal dive fee (US$3 per day or US$10 per year) goes toward the park's upkeep. Areas around the base of Petit Piton and Anse Chastanet bay are particularly stunning places to snorkel. The main **coral varieties** in St Lucian waters include the sizeable, tan-coloured elkhorn, pale yellow or white finger coral, rotund brain coral and the soft gorgonian type, coloured purple or green. **Fish** are plentiful, and the most

Watersports operators

Aquarius Water World & Rosemond's Trench Divers, *Marigot Beach Club* ✆451-4974 or 451-4420. Scuba, snorkelling, paddle-boating and Sunfish sailing boats.

Buddies Scuba, Vigie Marina, Castries ✆452-5288. Scuba and snorkelling.

Dolphin Divers, Rodney Bay ✆452-9485. Scuba and snorkelling.

Frog's Diving, *Jalousie Hilton Resort*, Soufrière ✆452-0913; *Windjammer Landing*, Labrellotte Bay ✆452-0913. Scuba, snorkelling, water-skiing, banana boat rides, windsurfing, kayaking and sailing.

Island Windsurfing, Anse de Sables, Vieux Fort ✆451-3000. Windsurfing.

Moorings Scuba, Marigot Bay ✆451-4357. Scuba and snorkelling.

Scuba St Lucia, *Anse Chastanet*, Soufrière ✆459-7755 or 459-7000. Scuba and snorkelling.

St Lucia Undersea Adventures, Vigie Cove, Castries ✆450-1640 or 450-7716. Scuba and snorkelling.

Waves, Choc Bay ✆451-3000. Sunfish, windsurfing and paddle-boating.

frequent reef visitors are anglefish (blue and yellow with darkish stripes), red squirrelfish, bright blue parrotfish, green or blue and yellow wrasses and the triggerfish, dark green with a yellow belly and an elongated snout.

Many of the island's diving centres rent masks and fins for about US$10 per hour, and will also take you out for an escorted off-shore trip, often a far more rewarding option than striking out alone from the beach. Trips cost US$20–35, including equipment and a guide who will take you to the best snorkel spots and point out things of interest.

WATERSPORTS OPERATORS

BOAT TRIPS

Gliding up and down St Lucia's accessible and calm west coast, **sightseeing** and **party boats** (usually customized catamarans) offer a great way to see the bays and interior mountain peaks from a different perspective. Most excursions include stops for snorkelling and swimming, or a visit to a coastal village (probably Soufrière or Marigot Bay) as well as lunch and drinks. However, you should bear in mind that as the boats are often crowded with rowdy revellers taking advantage of the free-flowing rum, the trip may not be the quiet cruise you might anticipate; if you're looking for a more sedate excursion, say so when you book. Most depart from Vigie Marina in Castries or the Rodney Bay Marina, and head south along the coast for full- or half-day cruises, which start at US$75 per person for the full day, and about US$40 for the half day; check whether transport to and from your hotel is included in the price.

Some of the best **cruise operators** include Endless Summer Cruises (℗450-8651), which runs full-day tours out of Rodney Bay to Soufrière's volcano and Diamond Falls, with stops at beaches around Anse Cochon for swimming and snorkelling, as well as sightseeing at Marigot Bay. They also operate half-day swimming jaunts to various spots along the northwest coast. Used in the filming of the movie *Roots*, the *Unicorn* (℗452-6811) is a 140-foot brig that looks like an old pirate ship and makes trips to Soufrière and the surrounding attractions, while the *Mango Tango* catamaran (℗452-0459) takes snorkellers out to various west coast spots. For a larger, all-inclusive tour that takes in Soufrière's active volcano and the Diamond waterfall and botanical gardens, with lunch at *Still Plantation*, call the motor-yacht company Vigie's Luxury Tours (℗452-8232).

YACHT CHARTERS

Sailing around St Lucia or visiting neighbouring islands aboard your own private yacht has become increasingly popular in recent years, and several companies in St Lucia will **charter a yacht**. Costs depend on the size of the group and the length of time you'll be sailing, and on the size of the yacht, but you can expect to pay anything from US$1600 per week in low season to US$6000 per week in high season. If you don't have sailing skills or you're after complete relaxation (and no work), a captain and crew or a cook can accompany you, but this will add considerably to the costs: a captain is roughly US$100 per day, a cook about US$50 per day, and a crew US$25 each per day. The larger charter companies can arrange complete packages which base your holiday around yachting, and include charter fees, airfares and hotel stays while the boat is prepared. Listed below are the most reliable operators.

Destination St Lucia, Rodney Bay ©452-8531.
Moorings Yacht Charters, Marigot Bay ©451-4357; in North America 888-922-4811.
Stirrup Yachts, Castries ©452-8000.

SPORTS FISHING

Sports fishing enthusiasts will find good game fishing off-shore of St Lucia, where the main catches include sizeable marlin, kingsfish, wahoo and shark. If you're lucky, you might also hook the rarer tuna, dorado or mackerel. Deep-sea fishing excursions run half or full days, with bait and tackle (and sometimes drinks) included; full-day trips include lunch. Half-days start at about US$300 for as many as six people. To arrange a trip, contact Captain Bravo at Marigot Bay (©451-4064), Captain Mike at Vigie Marina (©452-7044) or Mako Watersports at Rodney Bay (©452-0412).

YACHT CHARTERS, SPORTS FISHING

211

GYMS AND SPAS

When it's time to work off all that Creole conch and rum punch, try Body Inc. **gym** at the Gablewoods Mall (✆451-9744) or Jazzercise at nearby Vide Boutielle (✆451-6853). Both have workout equipment and aerobics classes and offer daily rates for visitors. The St Lucia Racquet Club (✆450-0106) also has a well-equipped gym with free weights, several Nautilus units and aerobics equipment such as treadmills, and they offer step classes daily. Entrance requires temporary membership – a rather hefty US$25 per day, US$80 per day for a family, with rates by the week or month.

After you've worked your body to a pulp, you can let someone else work to soothe it. The Royal Spa (✆452-9999) at the *Royal St Lucian* resort in Rodney Bay is open daily to non-guests for a wide range of **spa treatments**, from aromatherapy massages to facials and mud wraps. They also have a well-equipped fitness centre and a whirlpool bath and sauna. Treatments are charged on an individual basis and range from US$10 for an hour and a half in the sauna, to a pricey US$85 for a fifty-minute aromatherapy massage. Services are also available at *LeSPORT* hotel's Oasis spa (✆450-8551) and are somewhat cheaper than the *Royal*, starting at US$35 for a one-hour massage, US$25 for a facial. Other services include salt loofah rubs and seaweed wraps.

TENNIS AND SQUASH

Tennis is on offer at most hotels for as little as US$5 per hour, and at the public courts of the St Lucia Racquet Club at *Odyssey St Lucia* hotel in Cap Estate (✆450-0551 or 450-0106), where resident tennis pro John Easter provides lessons. The club has floodlit tennis courts, air-conditioned **squash** courts, a well-equipped gym and a well-stocked pro shop. Non-members can take temporary membership for US$25 per day or US$100 for a week; there's also a family rate of US$80 per day or US$250 per week. The St Lucia Yacht Club in Rodney Bay (℃452-8350) will let non-members use its squash courts for a fee.

HORSEBACK RIDING

Horseback riding is a great way to see the country, particularly the mountains or east coast where roads are poor and access by car is difficult. Most stables provide lessons as well as one- to four-hour rides, with transport to and from your hotel and possibly lunch included. Rides cost US$25–40 per hour.

In the **Gros Islet** area, try Trim's (℃450-8273), International (℃452-8139), or North Point (℃450-8853); in the **south**, contact *Fox Grove Inn* in Mon Repose (℃455-3271), just north of Vieux Fort, or Trekkers at Morne Coubaril Estate in Soufrière (℃459-7340).

GOLF

There are two nine-hole **golf courses** on the island: the St Lucia Golf and Country Club in Cap Estate (℃450-8523) is a public course, a par 36, and it's pretty adequate if a bit soggy during the rainy season; you play through twice for eighteen holes. Greens fees are US$21 for nine holes, US$27 for eighteen; golf club rental costs US$10, and carts from US$18. The all-inclusive *Sandals St Lucia* hotel in La Toc (℃452-3081) allows non-guests to play their nine-hole course for a fee of around US$20 for eighteen holes.

HIKING

Hiking through St Lucia's central rainforests and preserves is the best way to experience the island's fabulously beautiful **interior**; despite being laced by walkable trails, the mountains often go unexplored by beach devotees. You don't necessarily need guides for many of the hikes (though hiring one will help to identify local flora and fauna), but you do need advance permission from the Department of Forest and Lands (☎450-2231; see p.139) to enter protected areas such as the Edmund Forest Reserve, Des Cartiers Rainforest and the Barre de L'Isle area. Rangers, who serve as guides, are found at the head of the trails, and there is a small admission charge payable before you hike (see Chapter Seven).

Walks through off-shore **coastal preserves** such as the Fregate and Maria Islands nature reserves, as well as tours of the Morne Fortune historic area in Castries, are conducted by the St Lucia National Trust, who you can call for times and costs (☎452-5005; see p.33).

If you decide to hike, bear in mind that you'll be doing so in the tropical heat; wear light clothing and bring a hat, sunscreen and plenty of water. Sneakers are fine if you don't have walking shoes. For more on hiking practicalities, see p.139.

Directory

AIRLINES IN ST LUCIA Air Canada ℂ452-2550;
Air Jamaica ℂ453-6611; Air Martinique ℂ452-2463 or
453-6660; American Airlines ℂ454-6777; American Eagle
ℂ452-1820; BWIA ℂ452-3778 or 452-3789; HelenAir ℂ452-
1958; LIAT ℂ452-2348 or 452-3056.

BANKS Castries: Bank of Nova Scotia (Scotiabank), William
Peter Blvd; Barclays, Bridge St; Caribbean Banking
Corporation, Micoud St; CIBC, William Peter Blvd; National
Commercial Bank, Bridge St; Royal Bank of Canada, William
Peter Blvd; St Lucia Cooperative Bank, Bridge St. **Sunny
Acres**: Caribbean Banking Corporation, Gablewoods Mall.
Rodney Bay Marina: Barclays; National Commercial Bank;
Royal Bank of Canada. **Soufrière**: Barclays, Bridge St;
National Commercial Bank, Bridge St. **Vieux Fort**: Bank of
Nova Scotia (Scotiabank), New Dock Rd; Barclays, Bridge St;
National Commercial Bank, Clarke St; CIBC, Clarke St;
Royal Bank of Canada, New Dock Road; St Lucia
Cooperative Bank, Commercial St.

CUSTOMS On arrival, customs allow a duty-free quota of
one litre of spirits or wine, 200 cigarettes, 50 cigars and 250g
of tobacco. The first EC$250 in gifts brought in (which
includes the spirits and tobacco, but not personal effects) is

not subject to duty charges. It goes without saying that attempting to bring illegal drugs into St Lucia incurs severe penalties. For questions, call Customs ℂ454-6509. For customs information regarding your country of origin, contact the proper local authorities.

DEPARTURE TAX Departure tax is EC$40 (US$16) per person, payable at the airport. Try to have the exact sum, as ticket counter personnel do not always have change in currencies other than EC dollars.

ELECTRICITY The standard is 220 volts, although many hotels have 110-volt systems; these will sometimes carry a limited number of adapters for use by guests, but it's best to bring one yourself if you think you'll need it.

EMBASSIES AND CONSULATES British High Commission, 24 Micoud St, Castries ℂ452-2484; Organization of American States, Vigie, Castries ℂ452-4330. Australia and Canada are represented in Barbados: Australian High Commission, Bishop's Court Hill, St Michael, Barbados ℂ1-246 435-2834; Canadian High Commission, Lower Collymore Rock St, St Michael ℂ1-246 436-4950. New Zealand is not represented in the region.

EMERGENCIES For police dial ℂ999, for fire and ambulance dial ℂ911.

HOSPITALS Victoria Hospital in Castries (ℂ452-2421) is the island's main public facility and has a 24-hour emergency room. The private Tapion Hospital (ℂ459-2000) is on La Toc Rd south of the city. In Vieux Fort, call private teaching hospital St Judes (ℂ454-6684). There are smaller **medical centres** at Soufrière (ℂ459-7258) and Dennery (ℂ453-3310).

DIRECTORY: DEPARTURE TAX—HOSPITALS

LAUNDRIES Hotel laundries are expensive, charging as much as US$2–5 for short-sleeved shirts and US$3–6 for long pants or skirts. The self-service machines at U Wash N Dry on Darling St in Castries (℃451-7664) are less expensive. You can also drop off washing at So White Cleaners on Marie Therese St in Gros Islet (℃450-8808).

LIBRARY Each town has a small library, but the largest is the Central Library (℃452-2875) on Derek Walcott Square in Castries. Hours vary, but most open from Monday to Saturday between 10am and 1pm; several branches remain open until 6pm on selected days. To borrow books, visitors must leave a cash deposit of EC$40, which is refunded when books are returned.

MEASUREMENTS St Lucia is gradually transferring from imperial to metric. Some road signs are in miles, others in kilo-metres; petrol is sold by the litre, but fishermen weigh and sell their catch by the pound.

PHARMACIES In and around **Castries**, try Clarke and Company, Bridge St (℃452-2727) and Minvielle & Chastanet, Gablewoods Mall (℃451-7808). Clarke and Company also have a branch on Bridge St in **Soufrière**, and at JQ's Plaza in **Vieux Fort** (℃454-3761). Minvielle & Chastanet also have a Vieux Fort shop on New Dock Rd (℃454-3760). Most branches of Clarke and Company open on weekdays from 8am until 4pm, and until 12.30pm on Saturdays; Minvielle & Chastanet open from 8am to 6pm weekdays, and from 9am to 1pm on Saturdays.

PHOTOGRAPHY Prints and slides can be **developed** at Cadet's on Hospital Rd, south of downtown Castries (℃453-1446); they offer one-hour processing, as do Foto 1 Club on High St in Castries (℃453-0514), which also sells photographic supplies. Quality is usually good, but you'll pay more than at home. If you want to photograph St Lucian people, ask permission first.

TIME St Lucia is on Atlantic Standard Time, four hours behind Greenwich Mean Time and one hour ahead of Eastern Standard Time. No seasonal adjustments are made.

TIPPING AND TAXES Hotels add a ten percent service charge and an eight percent government tax on room charges, which may be included in the rates or added on to your final bill (see p.151). Restaurants often add a ten percent service charge, though feel free to add a further tip. Hotel porters and taxi drivers have come to expect 10–15 percent tips.

TRAVEL AGENTS Local travel agents can be useful for booking tours around the country and for scheduling trips to neighbouring islands or reconfirming flights. In Castries, contact Barnard's Travel on Bridge St (✆452-2214) or Carib Travel on Micoud St (✆452-2151). In Vieux Fort, try Global Travel on Clarke St (✆454-9040).

WATER St Lucia's tap water is good and safe to drink, but inexpensive bottled water is available from larger supermarkets.

WEDDINGS To get married in St Lucia, you must bring the originals of your passport, birth certificate and appropriate documentation if either partner has been divorced or is a widow/widower. Once on St Lucia, you must appoint a local solicitor to apply for a marriage licence, which will be issued after you have been on the island for two days; the application takes two business days to process, so in effect, you have to wait five days before you can tie the knot. Notarial fees and a marriage licence cost EC$402.50, registrar fees are EC$100, and a marriage certificate costs EC$8.

CONTEXTS

A brief history of St Lucia

St Lucia's first known inhabitants were the peaceful **Arawaks**, a race of fishermen and farmers who arrived from South America around 200 AD aboard dugout canoes. They settled in fertile plains adjacent to the sea or to rivers where they planted **tobacco** (which was used ritually), maize, **cassava** (the starchy staple of the tropics, which they called *yuca*), and **guava**, used as both a medicine and a food. Arawak paintings, or **petroglyphs**, have been found around Soufrière, the south and the southeast coasts of St Lucia, suggesting that these were the main areas in which the Arawaks settled; their language has also survived in words still used today, such as canoe, guava, barbecue, manatee and hurricane – "tobacco" is derived from the Arawak word for a pipe.

For more on petroglyph sites in St Lucia, see p.114.

The Arawaks' life on St Lucia was relatively stable until the arrival, between 800 and 1200 AD, of the bellicose **Caribs**, another seagoing group from South America who made their way up the Lesser Antilles chain in war canoes, capturing and destroying entire Arawak villages, murdering the men and making off with the women. The Caribs named St Lucia *Iouanalao* (also spelled *Iyanola*) or "Land of Iguanas", which later evolved to *Hiwanarau* and finally to Hewanorra, now employed as the name of the island's international airport. By the late fifteenth century, when the first European explorers arrived in the Caribbean, St Lucia had been inhabited by Caribs for over 200 years, and by the early sixteenth century, Caribs had driven off or slaughtered most of the island's Arawak population. The aggressive Carib presence dominated the region, and their reputation was far-reaching enough for the Spanish to name the entire

Caribbean Sea after them. Carib hostility had become the chief hindrance to European settlement of the Caribbean, and their barbarian reputation is probably behind the unproven assertion that they **ate** their adversaries.

European discovery and settlement

Unlike most other Caribbean islands, the European "discovery" of St Lucia is an ambiguous matter. Though it was long assumed that **Christopher Columbus** must have sighted St Lucia on his fourth and final voyage in 1502, no references to the island exist in his records, and it's unlikely that he ever saw St Lucia, let alone landed there. The island's name refers to St Lucie, an Italian saint whose feast day is December 13, and though this date was celebrated as "Discovery Day" for years, Columbus's logs indicate that he was nowhere near St Lucia on that day. It's most likely, though, that the first European to sight the island was indeed a Spaniard. Juan de la Cosa had sailed with Columbus on his first two voyages, and during an independent expedition of 1504, he sighted St Lucia and named it El Falcón on the maps he prepared. In 1511, the island appeared on a Spanish Royal Cedula of Population as St Lucia, and was included on a Vatican map of 1520.

As they did with many other islands in the region, the Spanish claimed St Lucia in absentia soon after de la Cosa's visit, but their attempts to establish settlements were swiftly repelled by the Caribs, and they made no great effort to colonize the island. In 1600, the **Dutch** made an abortive attempt to develop St Lucia as a reprovisioning stop-off for ships heading to the Americas or exploring the region. Their small **defence position** at the town now called Vieux Fort was destroyed by the Caribs, and they were expeditiously driven from the island.

The next Europeans to arrive on St Lucian shores did so by accident: in 1605, a **British** ship called the *Olive Branch* was blown off course on its way to Guyana, and its 67 settlers were forced to land on the south coast of St Lucia. Soon after negotiating with the Caribs for shelter, the settlers were attacked. A prolonged battle followed, and five weeks later, the nineteen surviving settlers escaped in Carib canoes. In 1639, a British group under the command of one Sir Thomas Warner arrived, but within two years, they too had been driven off. Similar clashes between Caribs and small bands of settlers continued for another dozen years, during which time the **French** were busy building up their Caribbean presence, and were able to claim St Lucia alongside several neighbouring islands with little opposition. They also established the **French West India Company**, a profit-making enterprise charged with regulating French mercantile enterprises in the New World.

French settlement and British challenge

The French West India Company often sub-chartered islands in its possession, and in 1651, St Lucia was **sold** to Governor du Parquet of neighbouring Martinique, who built a bastion on the peninsula to the north of Castries now called Vigie. The French made their settlement along a small creek which emptied into the bay at Vigie, which they called Le Carenage, and continued to battle with the Caribs until a **peace agreement** was signed in 1660. The cessation of Carib hostility allowed the French to consolidate their presence on St Lucia, but at the same time, the British were attempting to assert their supremacy throughout the region, and ownership of St Lucia became part of the wider battle to gain control of Caribbean islands. Over the next 150 years, prolonged and bloody Anglo-French **hostilities** saw the "Helen of the West Indies" change hands fourteen times.

The Caribs were also caught up in the struggle for sovereignty over St Lucia: both the French and the British used

Carib aggression to their advantage by employing them as **mercenaries**. At the same time, British and French **missionaries** were making great efforts to convert Caribs from their perceived heathen beliefs to Christianity. Nonconformers were often killed, and systematic annihilation (as well as mass suicides) continued until the Caribs could offer no further resistance, whereupon the British (during one of their periods of power) gathered most of them up and shipped them off to a reservation in Dominica, which remains the last bastion of true Caribs in the Caribbean.

In spite of the fighting, the French made the first concerted efforts to turn St Lucia into a money-making colony around this time, settling along the fertile southeast coast and establishing a **town** that they called Soufrière in 1743, and officially designating it the capital in 1746. By 1765, they had introduced **sugarcane**, setting up vast plantations and bringing in **slaves** from West Africa to tend the crops that they hoped would earn them huge profits. However, the British offensives throughout the next century prevented the sugar industry from becoming the major enterprise it was on nearby islands such as Barbados.

The British and the Brigands wage war

In retaliation for French support of the fledgling colonies in America's war of independence, the British initiated a prolonged attack against the French in 1778. After four years of fighting, Britain's **Admiral George Rodney** had established a bastion and a regional base for British ships at Pigeon Island, and from here, he launched an attack on French naval forces stationed at the nearby Iles des Saintes archipelago off the coast of Guadeloupe. The French navy was decimated, and British victory in what became known as the **Battle of the Saints** signified that French domination of the Caribbean was soon to end.

....

For more on Admiral Rodney, see p.84.

....

However, French control of St Lucia was not immediately relinquished. The 1783 Treaty of Paris put St Lucia into French hands once again, and the effect of the 1789-99 French Revolution was felt on the island when Republicans changed the face of St Lucia. All the towns were renamed, French nobles were executed by **guillotine**, and, in a radical move of solidarity, the Republicans **freed the slaves**. Noting the disarray caused by the revolution and sensing that the British would soon regain power, the Africans justly feared for their new-found freedom. While many stayed on the plantations, others formed a loosely knit freedom-fighting group known as the **Brigands**, who proceeded to launch attacks against the British, levelling plantations and terrorizing the island. In 1795, the Brigands captured Pigeon Island and held it for several weeks, but they were no match for British guns and military organization. Their numbers reduced and supplies exhausted, the rebels conceded defeat in 1798, striking a deal for their lives which saw them returned to slave labour.

Throughout the Brigand wars, fighting continued between the British and French, and the combination of Brigand attacks and colonial skirmishes saw most of the island's towns and villages razed to the ground. Many of the Anglo-French battles centred around possession of **Fort Charlotte**, the island's largest stockade, strategically placed in the Morne Fortune hills above the port of latter-day Castries. In 1796, the British launched a ferocious assault on French forces ensconced at the fort. After two days of solid fighting on steep hills, the Twenty Seventh Royal Inniskilling Fusiliers broke the French resolve, and the fort fell to the British, an important victory that represented the beginning of the end for French control over St Lucia.

THE BRITISH AND THE BRIGANDS WAGE WAR

St Lucia as a British colony

In 1814, the **Treaty of Paris** brought Anglo-French conflicts in the Caribbean to a long-overdue conclusion, with France ceding St Lucia to the British. Once the island was firmly established as a **crown colony**, St Lucian economics mirrored the pattern of slave-holding islands throughout the Caribbean. A brief period of prosperity followed the cessation of war, but this lasted only until the **abolition of slavery** in 1834. Though freed Africans were contracted to the plantations as indentured workers for a further four years, St Lucia's estates soon ceased to be profitable, and the economy crumbled.

Despite the economic problems, the nineteenth century did see the British attempt to assert their presence on an island still dominated by French culture, customs and language. English commercial law was introduced in 1827, and after being made a member of the British Windward Islands in 1838, St Lucia's seat of government moved to the crown colony of Barbados; four years later, English was officially established as the island's language. None of these changes did anything to improve the flagging economy, though, and economic prosperity didn't return until the 1860s, when the exceptional natural port at Castries helped to make St Lucia a primary **coal warehousing centre** where steamships called to refuel. East Indian workers were imported to shore up the depleted labour force, and the economy boomed for the next seventy-odd years. By the 1930s and 1940s, cheaper and more easily transportable diesel fuels had rendered the coaling industry obsolete, and St Lucia entered a period of economic decline once again. Financial disparity and discontent were swift to follow, and St Lucians hastened to form the island's first **trade unions**, which became the foundations of the political parties which later agitated for more influence over the government of their island.

By the late 1950s, the question of independence from Britain was looming, and small island nations such as St Lucia saw federalism as the most advantageous way forward. In 1958, St Lucia joined other British colonies in the West Indies Federation, a political grouping formed with the aim of winning independence. However, with new developments in their bauxite and oil industries, key members Jamaica and Trinidad and Tobago soon felt they were economically stable enough to stand alone, and their withdrawal, combined with petty rivalries between the members, saw the Federation weakened and finally dissolved in 1962. Despite the collapse of federalism, St Lucia was firmly on the road to independence, having been granted universal adult suffrage in 1951 and a new constitution in 1960. The constitution established an internal legislature in St Lucia, and the island's first political parties were quickly formed; by the time St Lucia was granted full self-government in 1967, a two-party system had developed, with the conservative, business-friendly United Workers Party (UWP) consolidating support and vying for power with the more liberal St Lucia Labour Party (SLP).

Independence

After years of lobbying, Britain finally acceded to the successive autonomy movements throughout the Caribbean and granted the new State of St Lucia **independence** on February 22, 1979; however, the island remains a Commonwealth country and a constitutional monarchy, with the British sovereign as the titular head of state, represented on the island by a governor general. Independence negotiations were fronted by the UWP under **John Compton**, a labour organizer who later became the main player of modern St Lucian politics. Despite Compton's central role, though, the party elected immediately after independence was the somewhat radical SLP. The Labour party were seen as the more progressive option, and the SLP's support for communist Cuba and Maurice Bishop's revolutionary government of Grenada matched the popular anti-Imperialist sentiment of the time. However, voters were still loyal to Compton, and the UWP gained a strong majority in the 1982 election and retained its post in both the 1987 and 1992 ballots. A period of economic stability ensued, with the new tourism industry flourishing and continuing to boost foreign exchange, but the UWP and its leader lost favour after 1995, when hurricanes resulted in decreased banana production, strikes and rifts within the UWP. Compton resigned as prime minister in 1996, but retained a cabinet seat, and was succeeded by Dr Vaughan Lewis, a former director-general of the Organization of Eastern Caribbean States. Weakened by the absence of Compton, the faltering UWP lost decisively in the general election of May 1997, when the SLP under Dr Kenny Anthony won all but one of the seventeen seats.

St Lucia today

Though relatively stable, the St Lucian **economy** has never been one of the region's strongest, and today, the island's number one foreign exchange earner is **tourism**, which contributes twelve percent of the GDP and employs one in three St Lucians of working age. **Agriculture** is the second-largest industry, and more than a third of the island's population (some 60,000 people) are involved in the cultivation of **bananas**, which earn forty percent of St Lucia's export dollars. As in most Caribbean islands, bananas are grown by small family operations who market their crop through cooperatives such as the St Lucia Banana Corporation.

Currently valued at US$8 billion worldwide, bananas are a valuable industry, but recent **trade disputes** look set to have a devastating effect upon the St Lucian industry and the economic health of the island as a whole. Disease and weighty production costs make it roughly three times more expensive to harvest Caribbean bananas than those grown in Latin America by more efficient US-based companies such as Chiquita, Dole and Del Monte. The main market for Caribbean bananas is the European Union (EU), and since the early 1990s, **special trading privileges** have been awarded to some seventy developing nations, mostly former British and French colonies in the African, Caribbean and Pacific (ACP) union; the EU has also imposed quotas and tariffs on Latin American producers and granted advantageous importation terms to European companies such as Geest and Fyffes, which market bananas in Europe via regional collectives.

The Web site of the Caribbean Banana Exporters Association (*www.cbea.org*) carries an up-to-date discussion of the current trade disputes.

Asserting that they had lost half of their UK sales, US-based banana producers responded to the preferential treatment in 1995 by **filing complaints** with the World Trade Organization, and a 1998 ruling agreed that the EU licensing and quota systems were discriminatory and did violate certain WTO laws. The EU responded by dispensing with individual country quotas and some import incentives, whilst still favouring ACP nations by guaranteeing a share of the market to the Caribbean. However, this didn't satisfy the US and its partners, and in early 1999, they **refiled motions** with the WTO. Despite vociferous opposition, St Lucian producers continue to wait on the next WTO ruling with bated breath. Though there have been efforts to diversify into alternative crops such as peppers, mangoes and coconuts, these are far less valuable than "green gold", and the removal of the EU regime would spell disaster for St Lucia and her neighbours.

Bananas aside, though, St Lucia's **future** looks increasingly bright. Tourism continues to grow, and revenues are regularly channelled back into the island, used to improve roads and upgrade sites of historical or ecological interest such as Fort Charlotte and Pointe Sable national park. In comparison to other "tourist playgrounds" in the Caribbean, St Lucia has measured the industry's development, limiting the number of fenced-off all-inclusives and insisting that visitors are not corralled off into resort enclaves. At heart, the island and its culture remain relatively unaffected by the more negative consequences of tourism, and St Lucia enters the new millennium with justly founded confidence.

Culture and language

In typical Caribbean fashion, the heart and soul of St Lucian **culture** is a syncretic amalgamation of the customs, languages, religions and societal norms of the island's French and British colonizers, and of the Africans that they brought with them.

Today's population of 158,000 is of predominantly African origin, and some ninety percent of St Lucians are Roman Catholic, with the remainder divided between Protestant and Anglican faiths. However, though Christian hymns are sung lustily enough to raise the church roofs each Sunday, St Lucia is also a society in which esoteric African traditions of magic and spiritualism survive. Carnival is the best example of this fusion of Christianity and ancient belief: one of the stock characters of costume parades is the moko jumbie, a wildly attired figure on stilts representing the spirit world.

A secretive, mystical practice that also has its roots in African ancestor worship, **obeah** is woven into the fabric of local life, despite the fact that it's ostensibly illegal. Not everyone in St Lucia practises obeah, or even condones it, but the more superstitious still call upon the obeahman – *gade* in Patois – to fix bad business partnerships and love gone awry, or to attempt the removal of jumbies (*zobis* to Patois speakers), bad-tempered spirits that vex the life of the common man. The obeahman does his work through ritualistic use of herbs, rums, tobacco, potions and archaic incantations, but as anti-obeah laws are still occasionally enforced, casual visitors are unlikely to come into contact with what remains an arcane practice.

Language is another aspect of St Lucian culture which shows African influence. Though African languages were suppressed as soon as slaves arrived on the island, French planters still needed to communicate with their workers, and gradually, the common language of **Patois** – also called Creole (*Kweyol*) – evolved, heavily laced with French as well as African and English grammar and vocabulary. Though St Lucia's official language is **English**, Patois is also spoken throughout the island, though it has only recently appeared in written form. Spellings, punctuation and word accents vary wildly as a result, and Patois remains most efficient, not to mention melodious, when spoken: several local radio and television programmes are conducted entirely in Patois. The structure and pronunciation rely heavily on French: the word for dinner is "*dine*", pronounced dee-NAY), while St Lucia becomes *Set Lisi*, a plantain is a "*banan*", sick is "*malad*" and please is "*su ple*". Mary W. Toynbee's *A Visitor's Guide to St Lucian Patois* (see Books, p.233) is an excellent reference guide to the lingua franca.

Books

Where possible, we've given publishers in both the UK and USA, in that order, for each of the books listed here. If only one publisher is listed, the country of publication is included.

If you're interested in delving into Caribbean fiction, it's well worth taking a look at the novels published by Macmillan's Caribbean publishing imprint.

Daryl Cumber Dance (ed), *Fifty Caribbean Writers: A Bio-bibliographical Critical Sourcebook* (Greenwood Press, US). Presents short biographies of important English-language Caribbean writers from 1700 until the 1980s.

Robert J. Devaux, *Pigeon Island National Landmark: A Brief History and Guide* (St Lucia National Trust). Colour pamphlet with the history of the island from Arawak to modern times.

Brian Dyde, *Caribbean Companion* (Caribbean Publishing, UK). A good, practical, A to Z reference guide to Caribbean terminology, history and personalities, presented in encyclopedia format.

Guy Ellis, *Saint Lucia, Helen of the West Indies* (Caribbean Publishing; Hunter Publishing). Short treatment of the history and background of the island, with excellent photographs.

Peter Evans, *Birds of the Eastern Caribbean* (Caribbean Publishing, UK). Lists nearly three hundred birds native to the Eastern Caribbean, with colour photos and charts to locate by island.

James Ferguson, *Far From Paradise – An Introduction to Caribbean Development* (Latin American Bureau, UK). A little outdated, but a solid, critical overview of regional economics.

Tighe Geoghegan and Yves Renard, *Maria Islands Nature Reserve* (St Lucia National Trust). Interpretive pamphlet to the flora and fauna of the small islands, with photographs, unfortunately in black and white.

Penelope N. Honychurch, *Caribbean Wild Plants and Their Uses* (Caribbean Publishing, UK). The author uses her own illustrations to help describe the uses of herbs and other plants in island folklore.

Eugene Kaplan, *Field Guide to the Coral Reefs of the Caribbean* (Houghton Mifflin). Useful introduction to everything you'll find under the sea in St Lucia.

Pamela Mordecai and Betty Wilson (eds), *Her True True Name* (Caribbean Publishing, UK). Absorbing collection of short stories by women writers from the Caribbean.

J.P. Parry, Philip Sherlock & Anthony Maingot, *A Short History of the West Indies* (Caribbean Publishing, UK). The best concise history of the region, taking the story up on the mid-1980s and good on general issues like regional cooperation and debt crisis.

Polly Pattullo, *Last Resorts – The Cost of Tourism in the Caribbean* (Cassell, UK). Important and well-researched critique of the tourist industry and its impact on the islands, with many references to St Lucia.

Bob Shacochis, *Easy in the Islands* (Picador; Penguin). A collection of short stories that centres on life in the islands and was winner of the American Book Award.

P.D. Stiling, *Butterflies and Other Insects of the Eastern Caribbean* (Caribbean Publishing, UK). Contains photographs and detailed descriptions.

Mary W. Toynbee, *A Visitor's Guide to St Lucian Patois* (Lithographic Press, St Lucia). An easy-to-read reference guide, written in a light tone, with a dictionary, common phrases and short history of Patois etymology.

Derek Walcott, *Collected Poems 1948-1984* and *Omeros* (Faber & Faber; Noonday Press). The former provides a good overview of the Nobel Prize-winner's early work. A poem of exile and spiritual travel in the West Indies which utilizes the framework of Homer's *Iliad* and *Odyssey*, the cadence of the epic *Omeros* is purely West Indian.

John Noble Wilford, *The Mysterious History of Columbus: An Exploration of the Man, the Myth, the Legacy* (Alfred A. Knopf, US). A recent treatment of the vain, enigmatic and somewhat failed man who commenced European involvement in the West Indies.

Herman Wouk, *Don't Stop the Carnival* (Harper Collins; Little, Brown & Co). Lively, humorous but slightly dated tale of a Broadway publicity agent who buys a small inn on a Caribbean island.

INDEX

Stay in touch with us!

ROUGH*NEWS* **is Rough Guides' free
newsletter.
In four issues a year we give you
news, travel issues, music reviews,
readers' letters and the latest
dispatches from authors on the road.**

I would like to receive ROUGH*NEWS*: please put me on your free mailing list.

NAME . . . .

ADDRESS . . . .

Please clip or photocopy and send to: Rough Guides, 62-70 Shorts Gardens,
London WC2H 9AB, England

or Rough Guides, 375 Hudson Street, New York, NY 10014, USA.

ROUGH GUIDES: Travel

ROUGH GUIDES: Mini Guides, Travel Specials and Phrasebooks

MINI GUIDES

Antigua
Bangkok
Barbados
Big Island of Hawaii
Boston
Brussels
Budapest
Dublin
Edinburgh
Florence
Honolulu
Lisbon
London Restaurants
Madrid
Maui
Melbourne
New Orleans
St Lucia

Seattle
Sydney
Tokyo
Toronto

TRAVEL SPECIALS

First-Time Asia
First-Time Europe
More Women Travel

PHRASEBOOKS

Czech
Dutch
Egyptian Arabic
European
French

German
Greek
Hindi & Urdu
Hungarian
Indonesian
Italian
Japanese
Mandarin Chinese
Mexican Spanish
Polish
Portuguese
Russian
Spanish
Swahili
Thai
Turkish
Vietnamese

AVAILABLE AT ALL GOOD BOOKSHOPS

ROUGH GUIDES:
Reference and Music CDs

REFERENCE
Classical Music
Classical:
  100 Essential CDs
Drum'n'bass
House Music

World Music:
  100 Essential CDs
English Football
European Football
Internet
Millennium

**ROUGH GUIDE
MUSIC CDs**
Music of the Andes
Australian
  Aboriginal
Brazilian Music
Cajun & Zydeco
Classic Jazz
Music of Colombia
Cuban Music
Eastern Europe
Music of Egypt
English Roots
  Music
Flamenco
India & Pakistan
Irish Music
Music of Japan
Kenya & Tanzania
Native American
North African
Music of Portugal

Jazz
Music USA
Opera
Opera:
  100 Essential CDs
Reggae
Rock
Rock:
  100 Essential CDs
Techno
World Music

Reggae
Salsa
Scottish Music
South African
  Music
Music of Spain
Tango
Tex-Mex
West African Music
World Music
World Music Vol 2
Music of Zimbabwe

AVAILABLE AT ALL GOOD BOOKSHOPS

the perfect
getaway vehicle

for top quality, low cost, fully inclusive car rental in
over 4,000 locations worldwide. to hire your
perfect getaway vehicle call

reservations on:
0990 300 428
and quote ref RG

holiday
autos

the world's leading leisure car rental broker

MAP LIST

MAP SYMBOLS

═══	Road	Mangrove swamp
───	Waterway	Beach
Mountain range		Spring
▲	Mountain peak	Building
✈	Airport	Church
♦	Point of interest	◉ Restaurant or bar
Waterfall		⊠ Post office
Turtle nesting site		ⓘ Information office
National park or reserve		Cemetery

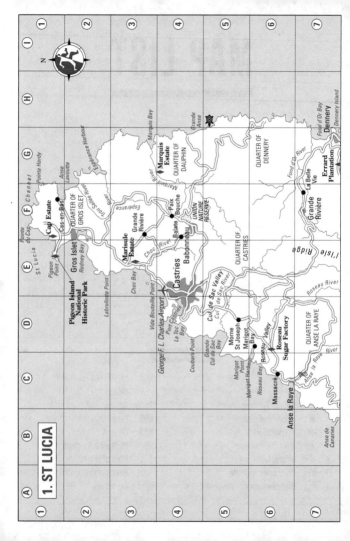

1. ST LUCIA

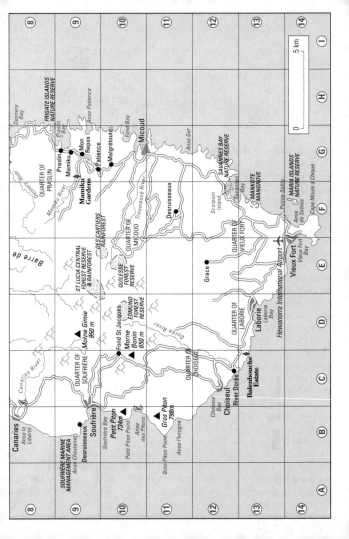

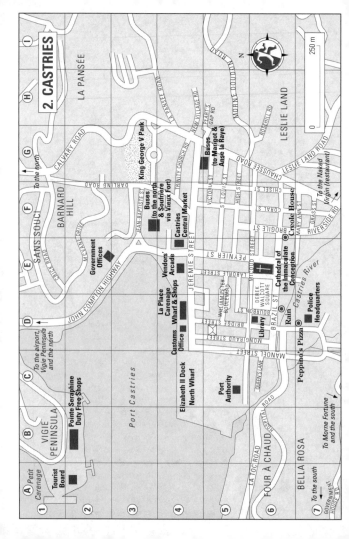

2. CASTRIES

LA PANSÉE

Petit Carenage

VIGIE PENINSULA

Tourist Board

Pointe Seraphine Duty Free Shops

To the airport, Vigie Peninsula and the north

Port Castries

SANS SOUCI

BARNARD HILL

CALVARY ROAD

BRICK ROAD

MCVANE DRIVE

JOHN COMPTON HIGHWAY

Government Offices

JEAN BAPTISTE ST

DARLING ROAD

King George V Park

LA TANSÉE ROAD

NEW VILLAGE RD

TRINITY CHURCH RD

PEARLS GAP RD

Buses (to Marigot & Anse là Raye)

ROSEHILL RD

CHAUSSÉE ROAD

LESLIE LAND ROAD

LESLIE LAND

Buses (to the north & Soufrière via Vieux Fort)

Castries Central Market

Vendors' Arcade

La Place Carenage Wharf & Shops

Customs Office

Elizabeth II Dock North Wharf

Port Authority

JEREMIE STREET

PEYNIER ST

LABORIE STREET

MICOUD STREET

BROGLIE ST

CHISEL ST

HIGH STREET

ST LOUIS ST

VICTORIA ST

CORAL ST

GRASS ST

MARY ANN ST

RIVERSIDE RD

Creole House

To the Naked Virgin (Restaurant)

Castries River

Cathedral of the Immaculate Conception

DEREK WALCOTT SQUARE

Library

Rain

Police Headquarters

Peppino's Pizza

SIR JAMES CHAMBETTE BOULEVARD

BRIDGE STREET

BRAZIL ST

BOURBON ST

MANOEL STREET

MONGIRAUD STREET

QUEEN'S LANE

HOSPITAL ROAD

LA TOC ROAD

FOUR À CHAUD

BELLA ROSA

To Morne Fortune and the south

To the south

GOVERNMENT HOUSE RD

To the north

N

0   250 m

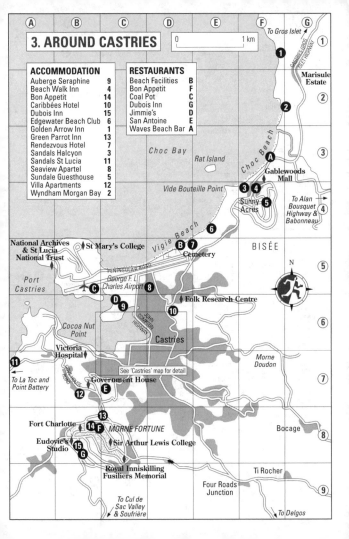

3. AROUND CASTRIES

0 — 1 km

To Gros Islet

Marisule Estate

Choc Bay

Rat Island

Choc Beach

Gablewoods Mall

Vide Bouteille Point

Sunny Acres

To Alan Bousquet Highway & Babonneau

Vigie Beach

BISÉE

National Archives & St Lucia National Trust

St Mary's College

PENINSULAR ROAD

Cemetery

Port Castries

George F. L. Charles Airport

Folk Research Centre

Cocoa Nut Point

JOHN COMPTON HIGHWAY

Castries

Victoria Hospital

See 'Castries' map for detail

Morne Doudon

To La Toc and Point Battery

Government House

Morne Fortune

Bocage

Fort Charlotte

Sir Arthur Lewis College

Eudovic's Studio

Royal Inniskilling Fusiliers Memorial

Ti Rocher

Four Roads Junction

To Cul de Sac Valley & Soufrière

To Delgos

N

ACCOMMODATION
Auberge Seraphine	9
Beach Walk Inn	4
Bon Appetit	14
Caribbées Hotel	10
Dubois Inn	15
Edgewater Beach Club	6
Golden Arrow Inn	1
Green Parrot Inn	13
Rendezvous Hotel	7
Sandals Halcyon	3
Sandals St Lucia	11
Seaview Apartel	8
Sundale Guesthouse	5
Villa Apartments	12
Wyndham Morgan Bay	2

RESTAURANTS
Beach Facilities	B
Bon Appetit	F
Coal Pot	C
Dubois Inn	G
Jimmie's	D
San Antoine	E
Waves Beach Bar	A

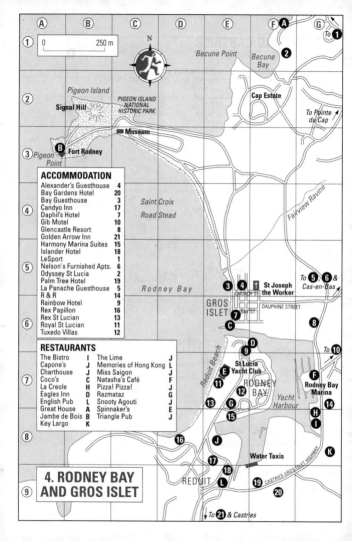

0   250 m

N

To **1**

Becune Point

Becune Bay

2

Cap Estate

To Pointe du Cap

Pigeon Island

PIGEON ISLAND NATIONAL HISTORIC PARK

Signal Hill

Museum

Pigeon Point

B Fort Rodney

Saint Croix Road Stead

Fairview Ravine

ACCOMMODATION

Alexander's Guesthouse	4
Bay Gardens Hotel	20
Bay Guesthouse	3
Candyo Inn	17
Daphil's Hotel	7
Gib Motel	10
Glencastle Resort	8
Golden Arrow Inn	21
Harmony Marina Suites	15
Islander Hotel	18
LeSport	1
Nelson's Furnished Apts.	6
Odyssey St Lucia	2
Palm Tree Hotel	19
La Panache Guesthouse	5
R & R	14
Rainbow Hotel	9
Rex Papillon	16
Rex St Lucian	13
Royal St Lucian	11
Tuxedo Villas	12

Rodney Bay

St Joseph the Worker

To **5** **6** & Cas-en-Bas

CHURCH ST

DAUPHINE STREET

GROS ISLET

BAY ST

C

8

To **10**

RESTAURANTS

The Bistro	I	The Lime	J
Capone's	J	Memories of Hong Kong	J
Charthouse	J	Miss Saigon	J
Coco's	C	Natasha's Café	F
La Creole	H	Pizza! Pizza!	J
Eagles Inn	D	Razmataz	J
English Pub	L	Snooty Agouti	G
Great House	A	Spinnaker's	E
Jambe de Bois	B	Triangle Pub	J
Key Largo	K		

Reduit Beach

St Lucia Yacht Club

D

E

11

9

RODNEY BAY

Rodney Bay Marina

F

12

Yacht Harbour

13

G

15

H

I

14

16

J

Water Taxis

17

18

L

REDUIT

19

CASTRIES–GROS ISLET HIGHWAY

K

20

To **21** & Castries

4. RODNEY BAY AND GROS ISLET

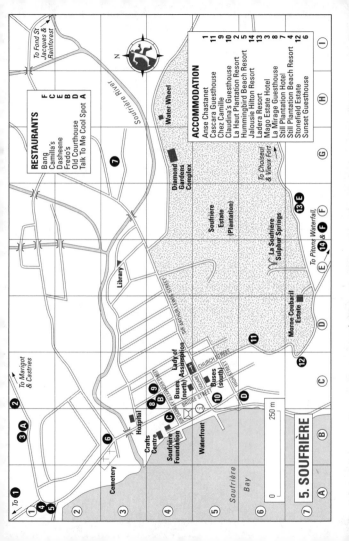

RESTAURANTS

Bang	F
Camilla's	C
Dasheene	E
Fredo's	B
Old Courthouse	D
Talk To Me Cool Spot	A

ACCOMMODATION

Anse Chastanet	1
Cascara Guesthouse	11
Chez Camille	9
Claudia's Guesthouse	10
La Haut Plantation Resort	2
Hummingbird Beach Resort	5
Jalousie Hilton Resort	14
Ladera Resort	13
Mago Estate Hotel	3
La Mirage Guesthouse	8
Still Plantation Hotel	7
Still Plantation Beach Resort	4
Stonefield Estate	12
Sunset Guesthouse	6

5. SOUFRIÈRE

0   250 m